CHLOE LUKASIAK

with Nancy Ohlin

Girl on Pointe

CHLOE'S GUIDE TO
TAKING ON THE WORLD

BLOOMSBURY

NEW YORK LONDON OXFORD NEW DELHI SYDNEY

This book is dedicated to everyone who was ever told that they weren't good enough.

Bloomsbury Children's
An imprint of Bloomsbury Publishing Plc

50 Bedford Square
London
WC1B 3DP
UK

1385 Broadway
New York
NY 10018
USA

www.bloomsbury.com

BLOOMSBURY and the Diana logo are trademarks of Bloomsbury Publishing Plc
First published in 2018 in the USA by Bloomsbury Publishing, New York
First published in Great Britain 2018

Copyright © Bloomsbury, 2018
Text © Chloe Lukasiak, 2018

Photographs courtesy of Kira Girard (page 12); Dawn Biery (page 13); John Zenone
(page 89); Camryn Bridges (page 124); YSBnow (page 149); and Oscar Skillar (page 196).
All other photographs courtesy of the Lukasiak family.

Chloe Lukasiak has asserted his/her right under the Copyright,
Designs and Patents Act, 1988, to be identified as Author of this work.

Every reasonable effort has been made to trace copyright holders of material reproduced in this book,
but if any have been inadvertently overlooked the publishers would be glad to hear from them.

British Library Cataloguing-in-Publication Data

A catalogue record for this book is available from the British Library.

ISBN
HB: 978 1 4088 9695 2
TPB: 978 1 4088 9825 3

2 4 6 8 10 9 7 5 3 1

Book design by Kay Petronio

Printed and bound in China by Leo Paper Products, Heshan, Guangdong

This book is produced using paper that is made from wood grown in managed, sustainable forests. It is natural, renewable
and recyclable. The logging and manufacturing processes conform to the environmental regulations of the country of origin.

To find out more about our authors and books visit www.bloomsbury.com. Here you will find extracts,
author interviews, details of forthcoming events and the option to sign up for our newsletters.

Hi there. I'm Chloe!
Here's a bunch of stuff most people don't know about me:

1. I used to be incredibly shy.

2. In elementary school, I would sit in the corner with a book and try to be invisible. At times, my only friends were my teachers.

3. In the past, I sought approval from my guy friends more than from my girl friends.

4. I fight with my mom.

5. I love rainy days.

6. I've had to deal with bullies.

7. I'm obsessed with reading.

8. I worry all the time.

9. I like to see a movie in the theater twice, and I'll go by myself if no one wants to go with me.

10. I'm a huge Star Wars and Marvel geek.

11. I'm a really competitive person (and proud of it!).

12. I have a brain that is constantly thinking and overthinking and analyzing.

13. I've always been scared of people making fun of me (including friends).

I'm also a big believer that everything happens for a reason. I know, I know . . . life would be way easier without problems and losses and disappointments. And medical issues (more on that later). But I wouldn't have achieved what I've achieved—my dancing, my time on the Lifetime reality show *Dance Moms*, my Teen Choice Award, my new acting career, writing this book (!!!) and so much more—without all the challenges I've faced.

So.

I'm here to tell you that you can achieve your dreams and goals. You can overcome your obstacles, whatever they are.

Because, all that bad stuff? It made you who you are; it made you stronger and wiser. It created the special nooks and crannies in your personality that make you *you*.

But if you feel like you have a long way to go before you get to "stronger and wiser" . . . or you're not super down with the nooks and crannies of your personality these days . . . well, I hope my story can help and inspire you a little.

In these pages, I'm going to share things I've never shared before—about my shyness and anxiety and self-doubt . . . about figuring out who I am and what I want to do for the rest of my life . . . about competition and friendship and family . . . and lots more. You'll find other things, too, like tips for pushing through a bad day (or week or month or year), my favourite charities, and how I celebrate my favourite time of year (hint: it involves pumpkin spice lattes). You might also find some drawings and poems and short stories by a certain someone, because, hey, it's all about getting out of our comfort zone and flexing new muscles, right?

Together, we will take on the world one pirouette at a time!

Hugs and kisses,

Chloe Lukasiak

P.S. You're probably wondering: what is a pirouette? Is it a Pokémon move, or a fancy French snack, or what? A pirouette is a dance turn that involves placing one foot on the opposite knee, toes pointed, and spinning around and around on the foot that's on the ground. It's one of my favourite dance steps because you're in control and not in control at the same time. It also involves a lot of falling on your butt while you're learning how to do it. Like life.

P.P.S. Will this book be full of dorky dance metaphors? You betcha!

Kiss selfie!
I should probably be doing
my schoolwork or folding
my laundry, but this is
waaay more fun!

Contents

CHAPTER 1

Back to the Future

From *Dance Moms* Season One. I'm the second one from the left—you know, the girl doing the oh-so-famous duck lips while everyone else is smiling. I obviously didn't get the memo. My teammates (from left) are: Paige Hyland, Maddie Ziegler, Brooke Hyland, Nia Sioux Frazier, and Mackenzie Ziegler (in front).

So I'm sitting at my super-cool white PBteen dressing table, which I use as a desk, trying to figure out where to begin my story. (Nope, that's not true. I'm actually lying on my bed in my sweatpants and my Ross and Rachel and Chandler and Monica and Phoebe and Joey T-shirt, eating raw Toll House cookie dough and stressing about my day.)

Maybe I should just dive right in.

I think I'll start with a few years ago and then jump back and forth in time—organized chaos, which is kinda how my brain works.

So in 2014, I said goodbye to *Dance Moms* and thought it was for good. I was thirteen years old. I had been on the show since I was like nine and a half (when I still slept with the bathroom light on, and I never wanted to be apart from my blue comfort blankie, Blue Kitty, or my golden retriever stuffed animal, Cami). *Dance Moms* was my past, and I had a different path ahead of me—a shiny, wonderful, yet-to-be-revealed path. A path that didn't involve fighting or social media trolls or the constant, constant pressure. I was sooo done with reality TV.

Then . . .

A few months ago, I found myself on the set of the *Dance Moms* Season Seven winter finale. Not to watch from the sidelines, but to go in front of the cameras and be part of the episode.

Why in the name of raw Toll House cookie dough had I agreed to this? (Uh-huh, you counted right . . . this is our second raw Toll House cookie dough reference, and we're only on page 11.) Was I forever stuck in 2014, dancing in place, unable to grand jeté forward into that shiny future?

That day as I walked onto the set with my mom, with the camera crew capturing my body language, my facial expression and my every

Mom and me on the set of *Dance Moms*.

move (I tried for my Confident Chloe Smile, like I totally knew what I was doing, which I totally didn't), I wondered if I could handle this. I was about to see my old teammates and also dancers I'd never met before. I never thought I would be back on set again.

Well, guess what?

It turned out I *could* handle it.

And I *wasn't* stuck in the past.

Because sometimes you have to go backwards to go forward.

I'll tell you more about that wild episode later on, and the other episodes I ended up filming after that, too.

OK, here's where I jump—I mean, grand jeté—way back to the beginning. Strap on your pointe shoes, people . . .

Nine-year-old me doing a grand jeté. I may look like I'm all "yeah, I got this!" But inside, my brain is churning: *Are my legs straight enough? Is my back leg higher than my front leg like it's supposed to be? Are my arms in the right position? Is my front foot pointy enough? aggghhh!*

IF YOU'VE NEVER SEEN *DANCE MOMS*

Dance Moms is a reality show on the Lifetime channel that debuted on 13th July 2011. It follows the young dancers on a junior elite competition team, our moms, and our coach and chief choreographer.

The episodes get up close and personal as the girls train for competitions and for professional dance careers. Sometimes, there are—um, how do I put this delicately?—arguments. Sometimes, the arguments get pretty loud and crazy. The moms really care about us daughters, and they're not afraid to show it. And the coaching can be tough.

Dance Moms used to be filmed mostly in Pittsburgh. In 2015, that switched to Los Angeles. As I write this, they're filming the second half of the seventh season. With me in it. And with a new coach. It's all so surreal.

CHAPTER 2

The Girl from Mars

I'm ready for my dinner now!

My full name is Chloe Elizabeth Lukasiak (pronounced loo-KAY-zee-ack). I was born on 25th May 2001, in Pittsburgh. The "Chloe" comes from a song (more on that in a sec). The "Elizabeth" comes from my great-grandma on my mom's side, Elizabeth Ulyas (whom I always considered to be my grandma, just as I always considered her husband, my great-grandpa Andrew, to be my grandpa, because they pretty much raised my mom).

My mom's name is Christi (which is short for Christina). My dad is Marc (short for Marcus), and my little sister is Clara. We live in Mars, Pennsylvania. Yup, Mars like the planet. In fact, there's a big silver spaceship in the town square. Our local high school is the home of the "Fightin' Planets".

Me, my namesake, grandma Elizabeth (Grammie Lizzie aka Gram), and cousin Greta.

We've lived in Mars since seventh grade. Before that, we lived in Churchill, Pennsylvania. (Both Mars and Churchill are close-ish to Pittsburgh.) My mom and dad got married pretty much right after college, and I was their surprise honeymoon baby. Our house in Churchill was their first home together. It was little and cute and had a picket fence, a wrap-around porch and a tree swing in the front garden.

From age three to five, I went to the Beulah Christian Preschool in Pittsburgh. I remember having friends there and being generally pretty happy. My mom happened to keep this big red construction paper thingy from my time there; on it is a list of nice words other kids in my class said about me. (Our teacher, Mrs. Thompson, had us do a project where everyone had to say something nice about everyone else.)

So here are my "reviews" (LOL) from the other kids and from Mrs. Thompson:

ABOUT CHLOE

CATHERINE: "She's a really good friend."

OWEN: "She is a good friend."

ANDREW: "A good friend and she's special to me."

JAKE: "She is cute."

CALEB: "She is good at making friends."

HUNTER: "Is good company."

SEAN M.: "A nice friend."

The other SEAN M.: "Is very pretty."

BRANDON: "She smiles a lot."

JACOB: "Is a good dresser."

HALEY: "She has nice hair."

ALAINA: "Good at playing."

MRS. THOMPSON: "Chloe is a sweet girl whose smile brightens the room."

I'm smiling now as I reread this list—not a bright smile but a wistful one. Because things kind of went downhill for me socially after preschool.

I morphed into Super Shy Girl in kindergarten (St. Maurice, Pittsburgh) and elementary school (Environmental Charter School, same). During lunch, I would sit in the corner of the cafeteria by myself, reading a book and avoiding eye contact with the other kids.

It was my shyness that made me act this way, but it was something else, too. Elementary school wasn't all red construction paper projects with warm, fuzzy compliments. There were mean kids. Here is just one example. When I was in fifth grade, I learned halfway through the year that my teacher was leaving to become a head teacher at another school and that we were getting a replacement teacher any day. When I heard this, I started to cry because I was going to miss him—he had always been one of my favourite teachers—and because who was the new person going to be? Would he or she be as nice as my current teacher? As I

"CHLOE DANCER"

This is how I got my name.
When my mom and dad were first dating, he told her that if they ever got married and had a kid, that kid would be a girl named Chloe, after a song he'd loved since age fifteen: "Chloe Dancer" by the band Mother Love Bone. Mom was like, "Whoa, excuse me, what? Marriage?" (They were on their third or fourth date or something.) Dad also said that Future Chloe would have curly blonde hair and brown eyes, which I guess means he has superhero-mystical-magical powers, since yours truly was born with curly blonde hair and brown eyes. And because yours truly ended up being a dancer.
It was destiny.

One of my early masterpieces, LOL!

MY OTHER
NAMES

I have a couple of nicknames: Chlo and Chlobird. The first one is basically short for Chloe. As for the second one . . . well, before my parents were married, my dad called my mom Bird because he thought she was like a clumsy bird. (Clearly my parents have a super-loving relationship . . . Ha ha, OK, they do, they're just silly!) When I was born, my dad said I was like the baby bird of the (clumsy) mom bird. And my sister's nickname is "Clarbear" (the "Clar" and "bear" syllables rhyme), so I guess my family has a thing for animal nicknames!

It's a Birthday!
The big 1!

Please join us as we celebrate
Chloe's big day.
Saturday, May 25, 2002

My first birthday!
Look at me rocking
that blue headband!

was crying, this girl looked at me and said, "Oh my gosh, you're being a crybaby. Would you stop crying already?" This made me feel so bad that I just cried harder.

Instead of ignoring the mean kids and just having a good time with the not-mean kids, I withdrew. I felt scared inside and tried to hide in the shadows. I figured it was better to be alone and invisible and safely sequestered behind the latest Sisters Grimm novel.

When I *did* come out of my shell, it was often to talk to adults. At times, my friends tended to be teachers, not other kids; for the most part, adults were kinder, more mature, and less inclined to pick on me (although there were exceptions).

Don't get me wrong . . . I *did* have friends my own age, and I was invited to playdates and stuff. It did take me a few months to establish new friendships, though. In fifth grade, I got to be good friends with these two girls named Marissa and Tehla. (Hi, Marissa and Tehla!) I also had my friends I danced with.

But those bullies at my school definitely affected my general demeanour big time. And in middle school and high school, I encountered more (and more powerful) bullies.

I'll talk more about bullying later in the book, because it's such an important topic and we need to have a serious conversation about it.

Luckily, things shifted back for me when I transferred to the Creative and Performing Arts School (CAPA) in Pittsburgh in sixth grade.

My second birthday. Mom is protecting my two little birthday candles from the wind (because that's what Mom does for me . . . every day).

Even when I was younger and had a hard time making new friends, I always had my family. This is my cousin Kate and me at Disney World, wearing matching dresses my mom made us.

(When I received my acceptance letter, I screamed with joy—you know, the way people do when they get that letter from the college of their dreams and it's like: *yaaay!*) At CAPA, there was nowhere to hide; it was loud and boisterous, full of singing and dancing and drama and musical theatre and absolutely *buzzing* with creative energy. Everyone had to be *on*—no introverts allowed—but at the same time, everyone was accepted and supported. This amazing (and fun!) environment nudged me out of my shell. I became more talkative and extroverted; it became much easier for me to make friends my own age.

But all this came to a screeching halt when we moved to Mars to be closer to my dad's work and I transferred to the middle school there. I was so nervous because it wasn't a performing arts school like CAPA. I also dreaded having to make new friends. What if I didn't fit in? What if no one liked me? What if my clothes were all wrong and people teased me about my outfits? After my wonderful year at CAPA, I felt like I was back to square one.

MY FAVORITE

THINGS

When I was in kindergarten, my teacher had us fill out a "My Favourite Things" questionnaire. Check out my answers!

The person I most admire: MY PARENTS

My favourite book: DORA

My favourite movie: LITTLE MERMAID

My favourite TV show: DISNEY

When I grow up I want to be: A MOTHER

My favourite class: ART

My favourite time of day: LUNCH

My favourite season of the year: CHRISTMAS

The thing I do best: DANCE

To my surprise, I *did* end up making friends at the Mars middle school. (Hi, Marnie, Megan, Nicole and Sydney!) We were really close during seventh and eighth grades. But in ninth grade, I decided to homeschool rather than attend the Mars high school with my classmates. I came to that decision because I was travelling so much for my dancing and acting and other obligations. I had other reasons, too, which I'll explain in that conversation I promised you about bullies. Unfortunately, though, doing all my classes online made—*makes*—it difficult to maintain those school-based friendships, which I'm sad about.

- I had braces from second grade until fourth grade, and again from ages eleven to thirteen. The first time around, I changed the colour every few weeks. I liked pink and blue a lot, and for holidays I would get into the holiday spirit (red and green for Christmas, black and orange for Halloween). The second time around, I decided to stick with clear (because I was older and in middle school and I had to be cool).

- When I grew up, I wanted to be a pirate, prima ballerina, author, Rockette, CIA agent, doctor, lawyer and/or marine biologist.

- After my *Little Mermaid* and *Dora* phase, my movie faves were *National Treasure*, *Pirates of the Caribbean* (speaking of pirates!) and *Alice in Wonderland* (the one with Johnny Depp). My top TV shows were *Hannah Montana*, *Wizards of Waverly Place* and *The Suite Life of Zack and Cody*.

- I loved making music videos with me and my friends in them, using an app called Video Star. My *Dance Moms* girls and I used to do this all the time. I made one just this last Christmas for my YouTube channel; my dance friends and I did "All I Want for Christmas Is You" (which was symbolic because, well, I'll tell you all about it in chapter 6). It was so much fun!

- Even though bows were practically a required accessory for dance competitions and recitals, I wasn't crazy about wearing them. And when I turned eleven, it was "goodbye, bows!" for me.

- When I was little, my favourite colour was red. Once my mom asked me why red, and I answered, "Because it's gutsy!" Now my favourite colour is blue, although I'm still a huge fan of red.

I look like a little old man waiting for my cup of coffee and my morning paper!

Still, I love my life in Mars. It's home.

I love our house, which we built three years ago when I was twelve. It's beautiful, and I feel very lucky to live there. What does it look like? Well, my mom is into interior design, so she had lots of fun decorating. The colour scheme is grey, black and white, and I must say, we have a LOT of pillows, lamps and sparkly things. Our basement is black and gold and full of Steelers and Penguins stuff. (We are all fans and watch the games together whenever we can.) There is a pool in the back garden with a pool house and a deck; underneath the deck is a little sitting area with loungey sofas.

Whew! Being a gourmet chef is hard work!

Clara's room is pink and blue and princess-themed. My room is black and white, although I may be redecorating and adding some colour soon if my mom will let me.

Oh, and I kind of have an unhealthy candle obsession. My room is full of scents 24/7. My favourites are lemon, lavender, jasmine, mimosa, cardamom, basil and neroli. I add special candles for the holidays—pumpkin, cinnamon, clove, apple and other autumn scents for Halloween and Thanksgiving, and pine, spruce, winterberry, gingerbread and spiced orange for Christmas.

Since I'm homeschooled, though, our house can seem very big and empty when the rest of my family is out and I'm at my computer writing papers or taking tests or whatever. When that happens, I just put on some music so I don't feel quite so alone. I also love to turn on the fire in the winter; it's so cosy.

(That being said, I'm 99.999999 percent sure my house is haunted! My parents tell me that I have an overactive imagination, but seriously, my door sometimes opens and closes by itself. I've also heard someone calling my name when my parents are sleeping.)

Anyway . . .

I have my favourite places to hang out in Mars. My family and I like this great restaurant called the Springfield Grille; my usual order is fillet of beef with broccoli and fries. They also have this really good bread they bring to the table—a corn and spice muffin—and I'm not joking when I say it tastes like autumn in a muffin. It is sooo yummy. (Best part . . . I thought they only served it in the autumn—because, you know, autumn in a muffin—but it turns out they serve it all year round. Now I often ask for a box of them to take home, and I eat them for breakfast and snacks.)

There is another local restaurant I like called Ichiban; whenever I have a shrimp and fried rice craving, I drag my mom or my friends there with me. (No eggs in my fried rice, because I'm a wee bit picky.) My friends and I also enjoy catching movies at Cranberry Cinemas.

Of course, what ultimately makes Mars so awesome—what makes it *home*—is my family. Home is wherever my mom and dad and sister are.

CHAPTER 3

Me, Myself & My Family

Dad with his girls.

My superheroes are Katniss Everdeen, Misty Copeland, and my mom and dad. Mostly my mom and dad. Without them, I wouldn't be where I am today. Even though we do argue (especially me and my mom . . . because that's what moms and daughters are supposed to do, right?). Oh, and did I mention my little sister, Clara? She and I never argue. (JK!)

I'm really fortunate because my family is very, very, extremely, humongously supportive of me. My mom is my best friend. She has been constantly at my side from the very beginning, taking me to endless dance classes and auditions and competitions, and then doing more of the same when she and I joined the *Dance Moms* cast in 2011 (except on camera, in front of millions of TV viewers, and with a whole lot of drama piled on top). These days, Mom literally flies across the country with me to Los Angeles several times a month so I can pursue my dreams—and while we're there, Dad holds down the fort at home with Clara and the laundry, the groceries, the school runs and everything else.

My best friend!

Dad works, too, at his job at the Children's Hospital of Pittsburgh of UPMC (University of Pittsburgh Medical Centre). He's the director of marketing and communications, which means he makes sure information about the hospital reaches the outside world. He has other duties, too, like arranging for celebrities to come to the hospital to visit the kids and attend fundraising events. He's great at what he does, and he works really hard. So does Mom. It boggles my mind that they somehow manage to do everything they do and are still such amazing parents to Clara and me.

They've been this way ever since I can remember. No matter how crazy busy their day-to-day might be, they're always there for the two of us—not just with the big stuff but the small stuff, too. My mom is my

A FEW OF MY FAVORITE FAMILY MEMORIES

⭐ When I was little, my mom would paint my nails, and each time before she started, she would say, "Welcome to Mommy's Beauty Shop! I'm Mommy. What can I do for you today?" And then she would paint my nails, usually red or pink, and add pretty little stickers to them (like flowers, stars or butterflies).

⭐ When I was *super* little, my mom would take me to Sandcastle Water Park near Pittsburgh, and she'd sit me on her lap while we did the lazy river ride. It was cosy and relaxing and thrilling, all at the same time!

⭐ The time my parents took me to Disney World for my fifth birthday is one of my favourite memories (and was basically the beginning of my lifelong obsession with Disney World).

⭐ When I was in second grade, my mom picked me up from school really early one day and said we had to go to the doctor. I started crying because I thought I had to have an injection; it felt like I was always having an injection whenever I went to the doctor. (Weird fact: I hated injections back then, but I love them now! It's a little odd, I know. For some reason, the idea of the medicine makes me feel healthy and strong and resilient, like, "Hey, I can do this!") But instead of driving to the doctor's office, Mom surprised me by taking me to see the *Nancy Drew* movie and then out to lunch. This is definitely one of my favourite memories!

✱ I love thinking about the times Dad and I played baseball in the street.

✱ On Sundays after dinner, Dad used to take Clara and me for frozen yoghurt at this place near our house called Mango Bean.

✱ On weekends, Dad and I would walk over to my school, which was like two minutes from our house, and he'd teach me how to play basketball on the outdoor court. In the winter, all four of us would walk over to the school with our sledges and whoosh down the big hill.

✱ BTW, I called my dad "Papa" until I was about ten years old. My sister still calls him that. (A little secret: I still call him that every once in a while!)

✱ When I was a kid, we would go visit Grammy Kathy and Papa D (my dad's parents) in the summer and swim in their pool and have BBQs. Aunt Kara, Uncle Jim and my cousins Emma, Katie and Dylan would also be there. (Everyone lived in Oil City, which is about an hour and a half away.) Emma is the youngest, so she and Clara often played together. Katie and I spent hours in the pool pretending to be mermaids and singing songs from *The Little Mermaid*. When we got older, we stopped being mermaids and started having swimming competitions with each other and with Dylan, too. It's so vivid for me, playing all day and then wrapping myself up in my cosy *Pirates of the Caribbean* towel and eating dinner outside with the whole family. It was always so joyful and fun and relaxed.

Best. Dad. Ever.

go-to for advice, especially with friend drama. My dad is very calm and rational, so I like to go to him if I'm upset about a situation and need guidance—for example, how to respond to a hater. And I can always turn to my sister when I need to relax or laugh or watch a fun, silly movie.

I also have a wonderful extended family of grandparents, aunts, uncles and cousins. They're all extremely supportive of me, too. I've always felt like I have to be "on" a lot, which is kind of a given when you're in the entertainment industry. But when I'm with my family doing homey things like having BBQs or celebrating the holidays, I can truly relax and be myself.

I know how incredibly lucky I am. Not everyone has a loving family, which breaks my heart. And many kids don't even *have* families, which breaks my heart even more. I am in awe of people who somehow manage to survive difficult childhoods and grow up to lead lives filled with love, friendships, fulfilling work, good health and all the other things everyone on this planet deserves.

There is this cool saying, "Bloom where you're planted". I was so, so blessed to have been planted in a beautiful garden with plenty of sunshine and rain. Yes, I have my problems and challenges. Yes, I have my awful, awful days when I don't want to get out of bed or I can't stop crying. But, big picture, I always have my family there to love me and support me, wipe away my tears and help me to find the "reset" button.

For those of you who don't have that . . . I'm sending you lots of hugs and encouragement through these pages. You're going to be OK. You're going to be better than OK. And it's my sincerest, most humble wish that my book might inspire you to grand jeté (or at least baby-step) into your shiny future.

And as for my family . . . I love you guys to the moon and back (and around the Milky Way galaxy and beyond). Without you, I wouldn't be able to take risks, have adventures and grow as a person. I wouldn't be *me*.

✳ At night before I go to bed, I always head down to the kitchen for a glass of water, and that's when I say goodnight to my dad. My mom puts my sister to bed, and then she comes into my room and we talk for a while before we say goodnight to each other. I love this bedtime routine; it's comforting to me.

✳ Every Friday, my parents go out to dinner. My sister always goes along. Sometimes I go, and sometimes I hang out with my friends instead, and sometimes I stay home and curl up in front of the TV with popcorn or a bowl of chocolate ice cream (which is like a double—or triple?—guilty pleasure). If it's cold out, I might make my famous hot chocolate, too—see recipe below!

✳ On Sundays, my mom and I often watch a movie together (like *Jaws*, *Saving Private Ryan*, *Jurassic Park*—you know, light stuff!) while she folds her laundry and I fold mine. But we never actually plan to do this—it just kind of happens.

✳ We like to play card games as a family (like Phase 10 and Skip-Bo). If we do teams, it's always Mom and Clara against Dad and me. If we don't do teams, Dad usually ends up winning, which is kind of frustrating because I'm really competitive—actually, we all are! Our game nights can get pretty intense. But we have fun.

✳ My mom's side of the family is Italian, so we like to eat a lot of Italian food—like pasta and pizzelles (which are thin, lacy, buttery, sugary, yummy-licious waffle cookies). My dad's side of the family is Polish, and one of our favourite dishes is called Polish Mistake (which is a mixture of hamburger, sausage, Velveeta cheese and Worcestershire sauce placed on top of rye or pumpernickel bread and grilled).

Two peas in a pod.

MY FAMOUS HOT
CHOCOLATE RECIPE

✿ Put a mug of milk in the microwave for about two minutes or until hot (but not scalding, burning hot!).

✿ Add TWO packets of hot chocolate mix (not just one).

✿ Add a LOT of whipped cream.

✿ Enjoy! It's super healthy. (JK! It *is* delicious, though!)

CHAPTER 4

Because My Sister Has to Have Her Own Chapter

Introducing Clara Alexandra Lukasiak, born August 17, 2009, at the Magee-Womens Hospital of UPMC in Pittsburgh. (My mom and I were both born there, too! Lukasiak women represent!)

I was an only child for eight years. I longed for a sister, someone to be with constantly. Once when my mom was talking on the phone, I yelled, "Elle! Stop it! Don't do that to the dog!" I wanted the person on the other end of the phone to think I had a sister. (I'm not sure where the name "Elle" came from. Improvisation, I guess! I must have been practising for my future acting career. We *did* have a dog, though, so I wasn't improvising about that . . .)

Right before Christmas 2008, I found out that I was going to have a baby brother or sister, and I was like *"Yaaay, best Christmas present ever!"* I went with my parents to my mom's ultrasound, which is when a doctor takes a photo of the inside of her body and can find out if a baby is a boy or a girl. My parents didn't want to know the gender, but I did. So I took a piece of paper, wrote down the words "BOY" and "GIRL", and put boxes next to them so the doctor could check one and secretly show me. When I saw what the doctor had checked, I began squealing and jumping up and down. I sure know how to keep a secret, don't I? Needless to say, my parents figured out that it was a girl!

They let me pick out her name (which was kind of risky—I mean, what if I'd chosen Backpack Lukasiak in honour of *Dora*?). Fortunately, I chose "Clara" after my favourite character in the *Nutcracker* ballet. (*The Nutcracker* has a special place in our family's Christmas tradition.) Her middle name is Alexandra; my parents wanted to give her an "A" name after Grandpa Andrew (who, BTW, is also known as Pappap).

Clara and I have a pretty typical big-sister, little-sister relationship. For one thing, we fight. A *lot*. We fight about silly stuff. We fight about everything and nothing.

At the Animator's Palate restaurant on the *Disney Wonder* cruise ship.

Can't wait to take her home!

We don't fight about clothes or shoes or such since we're eight years apart—she can't fit into my Nikes, and I can't fit into her itty-bitty Adidas. There's plenty of other things to fight about, though. I get mad at her for being in my business all the time and not giving me privacy. She gets mad at me for "tormenting" her. We fight if she's being a brat or I'm being a brat. (I know it's hard to believe, but I can be a brat sometimes!) Most of the time, what we fight about is trivial stuff, like what restaurant to go to or what movie to watch.

And OK, I admit, I sometimes push her buttons on purpose.

She definitely brings out the immature in me. I'm usually super mature when I'm out with my friends, at a dance class, on a set and just about everywhere else with everyone else. But with Clara, I revert to acting five years old.

For example . . . Clara has these adorable chubby cheeks and I like to squeeze them. This really annoys her, which makes me crack up, which makes me not want to stop. It's a vicious cycle!

Two Poems for Clara

by Chloe Lukasiak

I. SIMILE POEM

You have deep dimples and
your eyes are bright blue

You are like a teddy bear
I could just hug all day

Laughing and crying; your
laugh is the best

But we fight all the time,
that's what sisters do

I wouldn't trade you for
the world, I love you

Obviously, my sister and I fight a lot, but she is one of my favourite people in the whole world. Her laugh is hysterical and I've always loved her beautiful blue eyes and dimples. I've never been good at writing poems, so I wanted to challenge myself and write a poem using her as my inspiration.

Boyce Park in Pittsburgh.

II. METAPHOR POEM

You are the moon
and the sun

You twinkle and shine

Both good and bad

But never just one

OK, so I am a Gemini, which means that there are two sides to me (you know, the whole "twin" thing). When I wake up in the morning, my mom likes to ask me if I'm a good witch or a bad witch today. I always thought this was funny because I feel the same way about Clara. In the 2003 *Peter Pan* movie, one of the characters says that Tinker Bell is so little she has room for only one emotion at a time: anger or love or sadness, and so on. So that's where I came up with the lines "Both good and bad/But never just one". Clara is really little but she has room for multiple emotions—like she can be super happy and she can be super scary angry (on the level of Tinker Bell plotting Wendy's death by tricking the Lost Boys!).

Sisters at Disneyland for the InstaStory launch.

(InstaStory lets you post stories and videos that tell a story.)

Here's another example. So I'll grab something of hers—maybe her favourite blanket—not because I need that blanket, but because I know it will upset her. Which it does, and within seconds she's on her feet yelling, *"Don't touch my stuff!"* I'll go tearing down the hall shrieking and giggling and clutching the blanket in my arms. And she'll chase after me shouting: *"Give that back! You are in SO MUCH TROUBLE! I HATE you! MOMMMM! DADDDD!"*

Eventually, one of my parents will step in and try to negotiate peace. But it will be too late because by this point, Clara will be lying on the floor kicking and screaming, and I'll be sitting on her chest laughing in her face and waving the blanket in the air like a victory flag.

See, I told you . . . five years old. It's quite ridiculous.

Mom and Dad have told me (repeatedly) that I can't torture Clara like that because I'm fifteen and she's seven. I'm way older and way bigger. And I need to model good behaviour.

But it's sooo hard not to go totally Thor versus Loki with Clara.

Of course, who doesn't fight with their siblings?

On the flip side, I don't know what I'd do without her. She's my escape from everything, from the pressure. She's the person I go to when I'm completely overloaded and just need to relax. (Among other things, we like to sit and read books together.)

Clara and I are very different people, which may be why we clash *and* why we complement each other. I'm a big worrier and overthinker; she's confident and capable. I'm quiet; she's outgoing. I hold back on saying stuff; she has zero filter.

She's so interesting, too, because she can go from crazy little sister to responsible young lady, just like *that*. She can be super wild at home, but at school, she's a teacher's pet who follows all the rules and hands in all her homework on time. And she's only seven!

As for the fights, Clara and I are trying to figure out how to do less of that. Deep down, we really love each other and have each other's back, always.

The sisters chillin' at Huntington Beach in California.

Like when Mom gives us an order ("No snacks before dinnertime!"), and I catch Clara secretly eating popcorn, and she catches me secretly eating a brownie. We give each other these sneaky, wink-wink, "I won't tell Mom if you won't" looks. Because we're partners in crime. We're sisters.

SOME OF MY FAVORITE SISTERS (REAL AND FICTIONAL)

✷ Anna and Elsa from the movie *Frozen* (of course!)

✷ Katniss and Primrose from *The Hunger Games*

✷ Charlotte and Emily Brontë (because they wrote *Jane Eyre* and *Wuthering Heights*!)

✷ Beezus and Ramona from the *Ramona* books

✷ Sabrina and Daphne Grimm from *The Sisters Grimm* books

✷ Meg, Jo, Beth and Amy from *Little Women*

✷ Lena, Tibby, Bridget and Carmen from *The Sisterhood of the Travelling Pants* (no, the girls aren't technically sisters, but they have a sisterhood, so that counts, right?)

✷ And last but not least, my *Dance Moms* girls: Paige Hyland and Brooke Hyland, and Maddie Ziegler and Mackenzie Ziegler!

I try to imagine Clara and me in the future when we're all grown up. I don't know what she'll choose for a career (I don't even know what *I'll* choose for a career yet), but whatever it is, she'll be amazing at it. She can accomplish anything she puts her mind to.

Just a coupla American girls at the American Girl Cafe in New York City.

I can totally picture Clara and me living in the same city. Maybe we'll both live in Los Angeles. I'll be an actor, and she'll be an actor, too. I'll call my parents every morning, and I'll call Clara right after. She and I will meet for lunch or dinner or a movie or shopping (or all of the above!) at least once a week.

I wonder if we'll still be pushing each other's buttons then.

I hope so!

CHAPTER 5

Discovering Dance

Here I am after my debut dance recital in Pittsburgh, June 2004. I loved my flowers, the makeup, and staying up past my bedtime!

I don't know if I truly ever started dancing. I feel like I was dancing before I was even born (especially since I was named after the "Chloe Dancer" song and all).

My mom put me in a dance class when I was two because she thought every little girl should try it. She signed me up for a class at the same studio where my cousin Greta danced. In that first class, I remember us kids learning the basic positions for our feet and arms (first, second, third, fourth and fifth). Pretty good considering that some of us were still in nappies or pull-ups!

That year, I met my future bestie and *Dance Moms* teammate, Paige Hyland. (I met her big sister, Brooke, too.) At two, Paige was outgoing, silly and crazy (in a good way), pretty much the same as she is now. We used to hold hands during our dance class because we were so nervous about learning the steps. (My mom is reading over my shoulder and reminding me that sometimes, I would be SO nervous that I would just cry for the whole hour, and she would have to stay in the room with me. Yup, uh-huh, thanks for that memory, Mom!)

Nia Frazier joined the studio when I was four. Then Maddie and Mackenzie joined about a year later. I pretty much grew up with those girls and Paige and Brooke. (Kendall Vertes didn't join until the second season of *Dance Moms* in 2012, but she fit right in as though she'd been with us all along.)

SONGS I LOVE TO DANCE TO

Here is some of my favourite music to dance to.

✻ "Almost Lover" by A Fine Frenzy
✻ "Crazy in Love" (remix) by Beyoncé
✻ "Dancing on My Own" by Calum Scott
✻ "Don't Forget About Me" by Cloves
✻ "Skinny Love" by Birdy

DANCE STYLES

In case you're interested, here is a quick rundown of some popular dance styles. There are way more dance styles than I have listed here, but this will give you a few of the basics. (BTW, the terms "modern", "jazz", "lyrical" and "contemporary" are sometimes used interchangeably, but they are not the same thing!)

⭐ BALLET: Ballet started in Renaissance Italy, hundreds and hundreds of years ago. It evolved in the nineteenth century into the dance style we know today. Classical ballet involves music (which may seem obvious, but people didn't/don't always dance to music); graceful, fluid movements; precise steps and pointe work (more on that later).

⭐ MODERN: Modern dance was kind of a rebellion against classical ballet. It began in the early twentieth century, and it's more free-form than ballet.

⭐ JAZZ: Jazz dancing goes with jazz music and also mirrors its rhythms and techniques.

⭐ CONTEMPORARY: Contemporary dance developed in the mid-twentieth century. It borrows from both ballet and modern. It also has its own stuff going on (like sudden changes in rhythm, direction and speed).

⭐ LYRICAL: Lyrical dance blends ballet, modern, jazz, contemporary and other dance styles. The dancer flows gracefully from one movement to another and also expresses a lot of emotion through the movements.

There are tons of other dance styles—tap, musical theatre, hip-hop and swing, to name just a few.
Personally, my favourite to perform is lyrical. I love that with lyrical, I can dance my emotions. My other favourites to perform are jazz and contemporary.

I didn't really have an "aha" moment when I realized that dancing was My Thing, my number one talent. It was definitely a gradual process for me. I tried (emphasis on "tried") other extracurricular activities over the years, like piano, basketball and soccer. I remember a piano recital in second grade where I messed up the notes to "Baa, Baa, Black Sheep" and was totally mortified . . . like red-in-the-face mortified. I ended up hating basketball and was more than happy to spend the games on the bench. And soccer? I literally didn't know how to play or what was going on, ever. The one time I scored a goal, it turned out that I'd kicked the ball into the wrong goal. I had no clue, though; I was like, "Yay, I scored my first goal!" I leaped and danced down the field. I waved excitedly to my parents, who were watching; my mom smiled weakly and gave me an embarrassed little thumbs up while my dad covered his eyes with his hands.

Pink curlers before my debut dance recital in Pittsburgh, June 2004.

This is three-year-old me at my studio's annual dance concert in Pittsburgh.

Not that I was an expert dancer in those early years (and it still makes my head spin to think that I entered my first dance competition when I was five!). I wasn't one hundred percent committed to dance, either. In fact, when I was around seven, I began questioning if dance was even right for me. I hadn't *chosen* to do it; it had simply been a part of my life since I was two. And this thing-I-hadn't-chosen was eating up all my weekends and other free time. I was a little kid; I really just wanted to lie on the sofa and watch TV!

But my parents insisted that I finish out the year, so I stuck with it. I worked very hard with my teachers. Over the course of that year, something just . . . *clicked.* I spent the whole summer working on just my turns. Later, I devoted myself to my jumps and flexibility. As my technique grew, my love for dance grew, too. In 2009 I won my first national dance title in New York City: National Small Fry Miss Dance Educators of America. (I won for my musical theatre solo called "I Like to Fuss".) I was all in with dance.

That's how my passion for dance started. But just as my journey to "all in" had its bumps and obstacles, my journey after that was complicated, too—*more* complicated, because the stakes got higher.

For one thing, there was *Dance Moms*.

En pointe is the French term for dancing on the tips of your toes. There are special shoes for pointe work that are custom-fitted for your feet. The main components of pointe shoes are the *box*, which helps to support the toes, and the *shank*, which helps to support the arches.

I was nine years old when I first went *en pointe*. Normally, you can't do pointe work when you're really young because your ankles aren't strong enough. As soon as our family doctor said my ankles were good to go, I was fitted for my first pair of pointe shoes. I was SO EXCITED. For many years I'd watched, admired and envied the big girls who got to dance *en pointe*, and now it was my turn.

You may have heard or read about (or even experienced) the pain, blisters and general agony dancers experience when they first go *en pointe*. Those pretty pink shoes with the satiny ribbons *hurt*, and your ankles aren't used to supporting the weight of your body as you elevate onto your tippy toes for long periods of time.

But I don't remember the pain. I was way too excited to notice or care. I was finally one of the big girls! I was a real ballerina!

I worked hard and took a lot of classes with the older girls to build my ankles and get strong *en pointe*. I still do pointe work, although I've had to take time off recently because of ingrown toenails. (Sorry, TMI.)

Dancing *en pointe* is a whole other level of creative expression. You're doing this very, very difficult thing—dancing on your toes—while trying to make it look effortless and flowy and beautiful. With a particular ballet, you might be trying to tell a story (like with *The Nutcracker* or *Swan Lake*). Or you might be trying to express an emotion or mood or idea (like with *Glass Pieces* or *Concerto Barocco*). You have to be light as a feather, uplifted. And, unless you're going for a sad or mad or other not-happy vibe, you have to smile . . . and smile . . . and smile.

CHAPTER 6

Dance Moms:
✵ PART 1 ✵

Paige, Maddie, Nia, and I were getting ready to shoot the Lux "It's Like Summer" music video.

One night when I was nine, Paige and I were having a sleepover at my house. It was the holidays, and we were putting on a "show" for my mom. We'd dressed up in crazy, colourful costumes. We'd put our hair up in messy, floppy buns. We'd scooted the coffee table out of the living room to create a stage. My mom was the perfect audience, smiling and clapping and shouting "Brava!" (the girl version of "Bravo!") as we danced to "All I Want for Christmas Is You" and other holiday songs.

That's when the phone call came. My mom answered and spoke to the person on the other end for a long time. She kept putting her finger to her lips to shush Paige and me as we step-ball-changed across the living-room floor, giggle-singing and messing up the words.

Then Mom hung up and turned to us, a million emotions dancing across her face.

She told Paige and me that we were going to be on TV.

We were totally confused. TV? *No way*. Was this a joke?

Mom explained that a TV production company wanted to film the day-to-day of our dance studio, featuring the girls on the junior elite competition team. The cameras would follow us from Pittsburgh to various competitions around the country, including Nationals. It would be six episodes in total that would capture the real lives of us young dancers, our moms and our coach and head teacher.

Paige and I jumped up and down with excitement. We were gonna be TV stars!

This was the beginning of *Dance Moms*.

I had no idea what an incredible experience I was in for after my mom and I signed on to do the show. As soon as filming started (on 5th April, 2011, to be exact), my dance life went into overdrive. Mom and I began travelling every weekend to competitions, along with the other moms and girls. We had cameras following us around all the time (which was strange at first, but I eventually got used to it).

In some ways, though, my *Dance Moms* life wasn't a whole lot different from my pre-*Dance Moms* life. After all, I was attending the same dance studio I had always attended, dancing with my same teacher and with my same friends. I went to a regular school like a regular kid. The girls and I didn't walk red carpets or get special privileges.

A TYPICAL WEEK DURING FILMING
(SEASONS ONE TO FOUR)

MONDAYS
* We'd have a regular dance class; no filming.

TUESDAYS
* Pyramids. This was a new thing where the dancers' headshots were posted and ranked in a pyramid shape.
* We'd start learning our group dance for the upcoming weekend's competition.
* We filmed our interviews for the week.

WEDNESDAYS
* We'd continue with the group dance and get about halfway through.

THURSDAYS
* If anyone was doing a solo, duet or trio for the competition, they would get out of school early (off-camera). Once at the studio, we'd learn and rehearse the dances on camera.
* The rest of the day would be finishing up the group dance while our coach watched.

FRIDAYS
* We'd get on a bus or plane to travel to the competition.
* Once we got to our destination, we'd rehearse.

SATURDAYS
* Competition day!

SUNDAYS
* Home!

Paige and I were playing "crew." (It was 2012, and we were about to film a special for Dance Moms.)

It was a little weird when the episodes began airing, though. I was like: "Whoa, I can see myself on the TV *and* I can see myself in the mirror *at the same time*! And other people are seeing me on their TVs, too!" It was also weird to watch myself reacting or not reacting to what was happening. I remember this one day when there was this crazy fight. On the episode about that day, the scene just showed me with a blank expression on my face. But I can vividly remember a million thoughts and emotions were swirling through my head. There were other times when I would be crying on the episode, even though I couldn't remember crying at all that week.

After the first few episodes, I kind of stopped watching. For one thing, I was super busy with school and homework and the rest of my life! I also felt like, "I've already lived this—I don't need to see it again."

Back then, I didn't understand what a big deal it was to be on a TV show. I mean, I knew it was a big deal, but I didn't realize *how* big, I guess. I didn't understand, either, why people would scream and cheer when we showed up to places. I remember this one appearance with Maddie. It was at the Westchester Mall in September 2012; we were dancing at the East Coast Starz fashion show. (Fun fact: Maddie and I had choreographed our dance number by ourselves the day before.

On the plane.) There were like five thousand screaming, cheering fans. Confused, I turned to my mom and asked her what famous celebrity they were waiting for.

In any case, it was all good because I was with my friends and the moms I'd known since forever. We were seeing the country and spending time in cool cities. I got to dance *and* I got to have sleepovers in hotels. Not bad for a kid!

Looking back, my time on *Dance Moms* seems like a whirlwind of dancing . . . but also fighting. Anyone who's watched the show knows the adults on the show argued a lot. We girls were somewhat sheltered from the drama; one of the crew members, the talent wrangler, would try to distract us from arguments by saying, "OK, let's do school!" or suggesting some other activity.

Chloe Nguyen (a guest on our team that week), me, Mackenzie, Nia, Brooke, Paige, Maddie, and Kendall in our group dance "Why Not Me" in 2014.

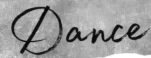

by Chloe Lukasiak

The song hummed to life,
lights awakening, heartbeat
slowing to match the music

Her movements started out
slow, almost as if she were
moving through water

But the music picked up,
her feet moved faster,
her heartbeat picking up
frantically

Suddenly she was dancing,
and turning, and jumping as
if the only thing that existed
was the music

Too soon, the music slowed,
her feet calming, but her
pulse still racing

She lifted her eyes to the
audience, victory enveloping
her whole.

Nia and me, 2012.

When I perform, I lose myself in the music and the dance. It's literally like nothing else in the world matters. And when it's over and I come back to reality, even if it wasn't my best performance, just the fact that I went onstage and opened myself up for everyone to see and to critique feels like victory enough.

Still, what TV viewers *didn't* see was the positive stuff that happened off-camera. They didn't see the moms and girls all getting along. We spent so much time together, went out for meals together, hung out. The girls were all friends, and the moms were all friends, too. Plus, the crew members were like our big brothers and sisters; they really looked out for us.

A FEW OF MY DANCE ROLE MODELS

* Misty Copeland
* Mikhail Baryshnikov
* Brittany Pent
* Kaitlyn Reiser
* Cheryl Burke
* Ryan Ramirez
* Any dancers from the movie Center Stage (especially Sascha Radetsky, Ethan Stiefel and Amanda Schull)

In any case, after the first season, we girls learned to make the most of the situation. Obviously, the show was high-stress and intense. Obviously, there was conflict. But we decided to ignore the bad; instead of listening to the fighting, we figured, "Let's just go have fun!" We had sleepovers. We made funny videos. We dressed up in goofy outfits. During the summers, we relaxed a bit because there was no school. During the holidays, we were one another's Secret Santas.

And speaking of holidays . . . one Halloween, we got back late from a competition. We hadn't had time to put together costumes, but we *did* have these pink jackets with our names on the back. So in lieu of Halloween costumes, we wore one another's jackets and went trick-or-treating. (I was either Brooke or Mackenzie or Maddie . . . I can't remember.) When we knocked on people's doors, they'd say to us, "Hey, aren't you the girls from *Dance Moms*?" And we'd say, "Yes, but we're also dressed as them for Halloween!"

Honestly, all of those girls were like my sisters. Paige was/is my twinnie. Maddie was a hard worker and also funny and sweet, plus we shared a dance brain (more on that later). Kendall was so nice and had this great laugh. Nia was a bookworm like me, so I could relate to her on a lot of levels. Vivi-Anne was very smart, and I always thought she was hilarious! Kalani and Asia were amazing dancers, too. Mackenzie was like my little sister, and I always felt protective of her. (She and Clara used to make trouble together!) Brooke was more like my big sister, and we became really close right before she left the show in Season Three.

I loved all the girls very much and consider myself lucky to have known each of them. One of my greatest honours as a dancer and as a person was sharing the *Dance Moms* journey with them . . .

. . . which has a Part Two.

Getting ready to take the stage for our group dance "Private Eyes" in 2013.

CHAPTER 7

What I Know about Bullies

Trying to be Zen and relaxed before my first surgery in 2014. (Nope, it's not working.)

When I was twelve going on thirteen, I noticed that my right eye had somehow become smaller than my left eye. My parents had noticed it, too, and took me to see the doctor. We thought he would tell us that I was suffering from amblyopia, commonly known as "lazy eye", and that I just needed some eye drops or whatever.

But my doctor said it wasn't lazy eye; it was something more serious. He referred me to a specialist, and I had to go through a tonne of tests, including a CT scan, an MRI and blood tests that involved having seventeen vials of blood drawn from my arm.

Then we had to wait a long, long time to get the test results.

Can I tell you guys how scared I was? I kept imagining the worst.

Well, it turned out to be a very rare condition called "silent sinus syndrome". The specialist explained that silent sinus syndrome causes facial asymmetry and can lead to long-term vision problems and other problems, too. Basically, when I hit puberty, one of my sinuses had got blocked and was pulling on my right eye, making it droop slightly.

I couldn't believe that I had this condition (because "very rare" means it's not supposed to happen to you, right?). The good news was, it was curable. In August 2014, I had a surgical procedure to clear out the blocked sinus. Then we had to wait a year to see if the procedure had taken care of the problem permanently.

It hadn't. I still had silent sinus syndrome. I met with three surgeons, and they decided that I needed a second operation to fix my eye. I had the operation in September 2015.

I then had to have a *third* operation in January 2016. They wanted to make sure that I wouldn't develop double vision as a result of silent sinus syndrome.

Needless to say, I went through a huge amount of mental, physical and emotional stress during those two years, from the time we noticed my eye issue to the third surgery. I remember that last operation pretty vividly. I woke up afterwards in the ICU. The morphine had started to wear off, and I'm being completely honest when I say that I was in the worst pain I had ever been in. I know it sounds kinda silly considering it's just this tiny part of my body—my eye—but it *huuurrt*. I couldn't focus on anything but that pain, and I couldn't stop crying, which only made my eye hurt more. Thank goodness my Momma Bear was right by my side the whole time, holding my hand while I sobbed, and waited for the medicine to kick in until I was OK again.

But do you know what? That awful, awful pain wasn't the worst part of the whole silent sinus syndrome odyssey. The surgeries weren't, either.

It was all the hurtful comments I got about my appearance.

I had encountered online haters before. But during that difficult time before I went public about my medical condition, people were actually cyberbullying me about my eye, teasing me, calling me "ugly". Honestly, I had to keep myself from responding to these strangers and posting: "I'm sitting here at the hospital getting seventeen vials of blood drawn, and you're calling me ugly because one of my eyes looks a little smaller than the other? You don't know anything about my life!" I knew that letting bullies get to me and engaging with them was a bad idea; still, it was *so hard* to keep quiet, turn the other cheek, take the high road.

It wasn't just cyberbullying, either. For some reason, some people I knew in real life thought it was OK to mock my eye issue on the set of the show. This absolutely devastated me.

Right before I went into my second surgery in September 2015, I decided to make a video so I could explain to the world about my eye and what I'd been going through. This pretty much stopped the online hate. People apologized, saying that they'd had no idea. And after

So many people have so much wisdom and support to offer on bullying. I've listed a bunch of resources and contact info. PLEASE REACH OUT, whether it's for you or someone you know.

(And of course, if you or someone you know is in danger, PLEASE CALL 999 IMMEDIATELY.)

24/7 HOTLINES (THESE ARE ALL FREE, PRIVATE, AND SAFE SPACES.)

✱ ChildLine: 0800 1111 (UK & ROI) or go to their website childline.co.uk to chat by phone or online, or send an email or ask for information

✱ Bullybusters: 0800 169 6928 or their website bullybusters.org.uk to chat, add a message to the message board or ask for information

✱ Samaritans: 116 123 or their website Samaritans.org provides information on suicide prevention, or you can email

✱ Bullying UK: 0808 800 2222 or their website bullying.co.uk for information

OTHER REALLY HELPFUL WEBSITES:

✱ The Facebook Bullying Prevention Hub: facebook.com/safety/bullying

✱ The Pacer Center's Teens Against Bullying: pacerteensagainstbullying.org

✱ Stopbullying.gov

The NSPCC: nspcc.org.uk/preventing-abuse/child-abuse-and-neglect/bullying-and-cyberbullying/

I'm lucky to have my family during tough times.

Me and my Hello Kitty after my second surgery in 2015.

the third surgery, my silent sinus syndrome was finally corrected for good.

Which brings me around to the all-important subject of How to Stop Bullies.

OK, I know what some of you may be thinking. Something along the lines of: "Well, Chloe, *I'm* getting bullied, and if I posted a video about that, I'd get like twelve hits, and nothing would change."

I hear you. I know that I was—that I *am*—lucky. The opportunities I've had in my life meant that my video could reach a big audience and shut down a lot of the malicious comments.

But there's a broader takeaway about bullying here, which is: *say something.*

If you're being bullied, don't keep it to yourself.

Tell a parent, a family friend, a teacher, a counsellor, the head teacher at your school or some other adult.

Tell a friend. Tell lots of friends.

Call the people at the ChildLine hotline (0800 1111) and tell *them*.

Or just take the first baby step by telling yourself.

Repeat after me:

I will not let bullies rule or ruin my life.

I am not what they say I am.

I am a good (or great or awesome or wonderful or all of the above) person.

This is not my fault. I didn't cause the bullying to happen.

Bullies do not define who you are—not even close. Their hate has nothing to do with you; it comes from a place of deep fear. Bullies are afraid—of life, of the world, of failing, of being powerless, of not being loved, of bullies and haters in their own lives. (Remember Lotso in *Toy Story 3*?) This *one thousand percent* does not excuse their behaviour. But this knowledge can give you at least some instinct about what makes bullies, bullies.

Also, if it's not you who is getting bullied but someone you know—maybe someone at your school or in your

BULLY: THE MOVIE

Bully is an important documentary by Sundance- and Emmy Award-winning film-maker Lee Hirsch. It has inspired an anti-bullying movement called "The BULLY Project". You can find more information about both at thebullyproject.com.

And while we're on the subject of movies about bullying, of course I have to give a shout-out to *Mean Girls* and also *Toy Story 3*, which I mentioned on the left.

BOOKS ABOUT BULLYING

Did I mention that I love to read? Here are some smart, powerful, excellent books about bullying (both fiction and non-fiction).

- ✻ *Blubber* by Judy Blume
- ✻ *The Bullying Workbook for Teens* by Raychelle Cassada Lohman and Julia V. Taylor
- *Bystander* by James Preller
- ✻ *Confessions of a Former Bully* by Trudy Ludwig
- ✻ *Dear Bully: Seventy Authors Tell Their Stories*, edited by Megan Kelley Hall and
- ✻ Carrie Jones
- ✻ *The Drama Years* by Haley Kilpatrick
- *Hate List* by Jennifer Brown
- ✻ *Odd Girl Speaks Out: Girls Write about Bullies, Cliques, Popularity, and Jealousy*
- ✻ by Rachel Simmons
- ✻ *Positive: A Memoir* by Paige Rawl
- *Thirteen Reasons Why* by Jay Asher (which is also a Netflix show)
- ✻ *The Truth about Truman School* by Dori Hillestad Butler
- *Wonder* by R. J. Palacio
- ✻
- ✻
- ✻

Before my third surgery in 2016. I was putting on my brave face, but inside I was pretty terrified.

neighbourhood—then the same applies. SAY SOMETHING. Bullying is never OK. It's not some annoying problem that should fade into the background of normal, like occasional breakouts or no Wi-Fi or the rising price of movie tickets. If we witness a person being bullied, even if it's a person we don't know very well or like very much or like at all, it's our duty as human beings to DO SOMETHING.

(Also, it's important to show kindness to people who are being bullied.

CHAPTER 8

Sticking with Your Dreams

Oh, did I mention I have a top-secret, super-private "Dream" journal that I carry with me wherever I go? This journal *might* include some ideas for a fantasy novel I want to write, with a heroine who—let's say—likes to dance and also read by the fire, and who might be fighting villains because she's super awesome and I kind of want to be her. The journal *might* also include lists of things that make me happy, some doodles here and there, some poems I've written, and quotes that inspire me (like the ones in this book!).

dream

my mom and I left *Dance Moms* in July 2014, at the end of Season Four. (Our last episode aired that October.) Many people have asked us why we left. Many people have asked us why we didn't leave sooner.

Let me see if I can explain, because it's . . . complicated.

So after four seasons, the show began to take its toll on me. The arguments I mentioned? It wasn't just the moms fighting anymore; the girls got involved, too. *I* got involved.

Also, after Paige and Brooke left the show in the middle of Season Four, I became the oldest and biggest girl in the cast. I'd gone through puberty. The others were smaller and shorter, and they could (for example) do a roll and get off the floor in about two seconds. It would take me a few seconds longer because I had to work harder to make my tall body move quickly. I had growing pains in my knees that kept me from doing certain moves (like jumping to our knees five times in a row). I was seen as too slow. People didn't seem to believe in me as a dancer anymore.

It was all really disheartening, and it crushed my spirit and my passion for dance. The show had become too intense for me—and for my mom, too. We talked about it and talked about it. We had a bunch of family meetings and discussions. In the end, Mom and I left the show.

It's never easy to walk away from something you've loved for so long, and from people you love. Life after *Dance Moms* was an ENORMOUS adjustment. And it wasn't just missing the girls, the dancing and the competing.

I also had these huge swathes of time, now that I wasn't on such a demanding schedule anymore. I had my life back . . . and ironically, I didn't know what to do with it! Sure, I got to hang out more with my non-*Dance Moms* friends, and I got to see more of my family, too. But

I'm not gonna lie . . . I became bored waaay faster than I thought I would. I saw a tonne of TV shows. I snacked constantly. All the changes made me anxious and a little depressed.

Mom gave me the rest of that year to decide if I wanted to continue with my dance career, away from the cameras. I took some time to think about it (in between binge-watching *The 100*, *Outlander* and *Game of Thrones* and eating a whole lotta raw Toll House cookie dough). I could have said no to more dance and ended that phase of my life.

But instead, I said yes.

I might have left the show, but I didn't want to quit my dreams of becoming—being—a dancer.

So the following January, I resumed my dance training at the Studio 19 Dance Complex in Mars. It was a big challenge to dance at a new place with new people. For so long, I had shared the stage with the same girls; we had been able to anticipate one another's every movement, every breath. I'd danced with some of them since I was two years old!

But I worked incredibly hard at Studio 19. I made new friends. And in the process, I began to reconnect with my love for dance.

During this time, dance studios from around the world were reaching out to me and inviting me to visit them. Suddenly, I was travelling and having the most amazing adventures. I ate macarons on top of the Eiffel Tower. I danced across London Bridge and on the stairs of the Sydney Opera House. I had my first kiss at the Blarney Stone in Ireland.

Let me clarify . . . I didn't kiss a *person* at the Blarney Stone.

Bonjour from Paris!

Check out who I found in this phone booth in London! LOL.

I kissed the Blarney Stone itself. Legend has it that you will have good luck if you do. But the whole thing was . . . *terrifying*. You walk into this huge, crumbling castle and climb up and up and up. At the top, there is a gorgeous view of mountains and forests. And then you go through these super-narrow passageways, and when you get to the actual stone, you have to lie down on your back and grab these three bars and scooch backwards, and half your body is basically hanging over air because there is a humongous gap between the stone and the edge of the castle. I was like, "I can't do this", and the guy in charge was like, "Yes, you can", and I started to cry. All the people behind me in the long, long line were getting very annoyed with me. Finally, I managed to stretch my body across the void and kiss the Blarney Stone. It was so wet and gross and not a magical experience at all.

Still, maybe it gave me good luck because my life after *Dance Moms* continued to be incredible. Fans never stopped reaching out to me. I felt so fortunate because here I was, no longer on TV, just a regular kid who happened to dance . . . and people all over the world were rooting for me and sending me their endless support. At one point I launched

WHEN I'M STUCK, I . . .

. . . read! Seriously, there is nothing I love more than curling up on my comfy chair beside the living-room window and reading a book by the fire. Especially if it's a Friday or Saturday and I have nothing to do, and I can just get lost in the warmth of the fire and the words on the page (and the sound of the rain, too, if it happens to be raining . . . Rainy days are my favourite!).

If I'm having a tough time trying to figure out my life, I find that it's good to just take a break and escape to another world—a wonderful, made-up, literary world. And if the book I'm reading happens to give me some life answers, well, icing on the cake!

Anyway, here are some of my favourite books—although the list will definitely be waaay longer by the time *this* book is published because I am *constantly* reading. No joke. You may notice a pattern—I love fantasy and romance and historical and dystopian fiction—except with the last two titles, which are in a league of their own!

- The *Throne of Glass* series by Sarah J. Maas
- *A Court of Thorns and Roses* by Sarah J. Maas
- *The Hunger Games* series by Suzanne Collins
- *The Sisters Grimm* series by Michael Buckley (I used to try to make my *Dance Moms* girls read them. And right now my sister is reading them.)
- The *Divergent* trilogy by Veronica Roth
- *The Red Queen* series by Victoria Aveyard
- *The Selection* series by Kiera Cass
- *The Shadow Queen* from the *Ravenspire* series by C. J. Redwine
- *Lord of the Flies* by William Golding
- *The Catcher in the Rye* by J. D. Salinger

AND HERE IS MY CURRENT TBR ("TO BE READ") LIST

(BTW, I'm ALWAYS taking suggestions if anyone has any!):

✿ *Flamecaster* from the *Shattered Realms* series by Cinda Williams Chima

✿ *Stealing Snow* by Danielle Paige

✿ *Six of Crows* by Leigh Bardugo

✿ *The Ring and the Crown* by Melissa de la Cruz

✿ *Three Dark Crowns* by Kendare Blake

✿ *And I Darken* by Kiersten White

my YouTube channel so I could keep in touch with everyone. (More on my YouTube channel later.) After so many years of being edited by someone else, I was in control . . . and it felt amazing.

Oh, and the Teen Choice Awards! In 2015, I won Choice Dancer (which was a brand-new category that had been voted into existence by the fans) because I received 30 million votes. *30. Million. Votes.* I can't begin to explain how honoured I felt (and still feel).

That might have been the second proudest moment of my life so far.

The first was the moment when I decided *not* to quit dance.

Now that I'm older, I have a little more perspective. I can look back on the whole *Dance Moms* experience with different eyes and (I hope!)

more maturity. I really do believe that everything happens for a reason. Sometimes these kinds of reasons don't reveal themselves immediately. It took me a while, but I know now that being on the show and walking away from the show were necessary parts of my crazy, wonderful, crazy (did I say "crazy" twice?) journey . . .

. . . as was returning. (But that's a whole other story for a different chapter.)

I want to leave you here with some wise words (or I'm going to give it my best shot, anyway!). So the thing about not quitting is this. It's not all cupcakes and roses and sparkly party banners that say: "CONGRATULATIONS ON NOT QUITTING! GOOD FOR YOU!"

Jason Derulo and Cat Deeley announced me as the winner and presented me with my surfboard at the Teen Choice Awards!

Mostly, not quitting means more of the same. It means more hard work and more pushing through the daily self-doubt. It means more trying and failing and trying again. (Remember my awkward pirouette/falling-on-your-butt metaphor at the beginning of this book?) It's hard to find your passion, but it's even harder to stick to it.

The difference is, you're in charge. You've made that difficult, all-important, exhilarating, Blarney-Stone-terrifying decision to stick with your dreams. You're in the driver's seat. Your future is *yours*.

And do you know what I have to say to that?

Congratulations on not quitting!

Good for you!

CHAPTER 9

What I Love (and Don't Love) about Social Media

Checking out a selfie with my makeup artist Mel at the Beautycon Festival in L.A.

$\mathcal{H}$ave you ever heard the following words from an adult in your life?

"You know, when I was your age, we didn't have Facebook or Twitter or Chatsnap, Snapchat, whatever you kids call it. Don't young people have real conversations anymore?"

It's weird for me to think that there was a time when social media didn't exist. For me (and my friends and just about every teenager I know), Twitter and Instagram and other forms of social media are how we *have* conversations. Yes, we hang out in person and talk on the phone and video chat, too. But our computers, phones, tablets and other devices enable us to connect anytime, *from* anywhere, *to* anywhere. I can (for example) send a tweet to my friend in Sydney, Australia, on a Friday night, and it will reach him seconds later across multiple time zones, just as he's sitting down to his pikelet pancakes on Saturday morning (and his response tweet might even include a photo of said pikelets). Go, technology!

Red lips x 2. A girl's gotta coordinate when she's Snapchatting, right?

Yes, yes, I know—social media has its negatives. I've lived them, and I'm sure many of you have, too. My parents (who used to help me run all my accounts) like to talk to me in that parental "we're just trying to protect you, honey" way about posting messages, photos, videos,

MY PARENTS AND
SOCIAL MEDIA

My parents used to help me with my social media accounts, but they've pretty much stopped because I'm older. They're still sort of involved, but they let me do my thing because they trust me. They know that all I'm posting on Instagram is maybe outfits or sunset pictures or selfies, and on Twitter, just relatable (I hope!) tweets. My mom also has to run her own accounts and Clara's, too. Still, she and Dad definitely check in on my social media; they also help me with mean comments and haters if I can't ignore them or handle them myself.

Must send out one last tweet before takeoff!

anything. They remind me that none of that stuff is private. Once it's "out there", it's public, and I can't totally control who reads it, sees it, hears it, shares it, quotes it or criticizes it. Also, it means I'm opening the door to "conversations" not just with my friends but with strangers— including haters and trolls (like the ones who made fun of my eye).

I still want to be out there, though. Despite the negatives, despite the risks, social media is really important to me both personally and professionally. It's personal because I'm a normal teenager and I like to be connected to my friends and to the world at large—like current events (anything that's happening in the United States and elsewhere), news regarding the entertainment industry (like new shows coming out, celeb drama and all that fun stuff), and movie trailers (but not movie reviews so much because everyone has their own opinion, so I just find these reviews silly). It's professional because this is what I do. As a dancer, actor, model, spokesperson, media influencer and now author, it's my job to be present and to represent on social media.

Another common criticism of social media, and of the Internet in general, is that teens (and kids and adults, too) can spend waaay too much time on their devices and forget about, say, homework or work-work or their friends and families or their basic daily maintenance like eating and showering. I get that. Fortunately (or unfortunately?), my life is so crazy busy that I have to organize my time carefully. I don't have the freedom to lose myself in marathon online shoe shopping or binge-watching bloopers from funny shows and videos of people falling or getting pranked. (Although when I'm on holiday or having a sick day, all bets are off!)

As for my YouTube channel . . . well, I mentioned before that I started it after I left *Dance Moms* so I could stay in touch with everyone. I also wanted to offer some behind-the-scenes glimpses into my life—the day-to-day as well as special occasions. Some of those first videos were a little rough! I didn't have the right camera, and I wasn't "in the flow" with making videos. But that's OK, because social media is all about being yourself! So it didn't matter that these videos weren't perfect; what mattered was that I was connecting with my wonderful, beautiful supporters! I make videos whenever I have the time, and I really love it. It's the closest thing I have to talking to all of you guys—like *really* talking—on a regular basis. There are some good moments . . . like when I let my little sister give me a makeover. Or when my mom imitated the

CHAPTER 10

In Search of (Self) Acceptance

I figured out a way to have my cake and eat it, too.

I'm a really insecure person. I mean, I know lots of people say this about themselves. But I'm *super* insecure. Like Bridget Jones and Bella Swan insecure. Like the narrator from Daphne du Maurier's *Rebecca* insecure. Like the shy rainbow from *Dora the Explorer* and Piglet from *Winnie-the-Pooh* and Violet from *The Incredibles* insecure.

Now, imagine all this insecurity rolled up into one person, and that's me in a nutshell. Not to be dramatic about it, but it's true.

I've been like this since I was little. In some ways, it makes no sense because I was (and continue to be) very, very loved by my parents, and they raised me to feel good about myself and proud of myself, no matter what.

So why am I insecure?

PERFORMANCE (UN)ANXIETY

Since I have become a more confident dancer, I've learned how to handle memory slips and other dance mishaps more, um, gracefully. For one thing, I've learned to improvise really well. So if I forget my steps or execute the wrong steps, I can on the spot come up with a swatch of new choreography to fix the problem. Also, I'm better about not making an "Oops, I just messed up!" face. I try, no matter how badly things are falling apart, to smile and smile and smile like I know exactly what I'm doing.

I also have some new habits and rituals for before I step onto the stage. Say I'm in a group number at a competition. Before we go on, we'll run through our number once together. We also do the Eight-Count Ritual (which I'll tell you more about later).

Then I'll go off by myself and run through the number a couple of times on my own.

Then I'll do some deep breathing.

Then I'll give myself that pep talk about my parents and the sun coming up and so forth.

Then I'll remind myself that when I get out there, I need to focus on my dancing and my choreography, not the audience.

Then I'm ready to go.

The Child

by Chloe Lukasiak

I.

The child loved the stars.

They were a sign that something beautiful could light
up the darkness.

Darkness surrounded the child, but she did not mind,
so long as she had her stars.

They made her feel small and insignificant, yet so very alive,

Alive in ways that were incomprehensible to most people.

People lived, but not like this child.

II.

Each day was a battle for the child.

But in the daytime, she would think about the stars, how
she would be enveloped by their beauty and compassion once
the darkness came.

Night was a time of peace and calm for everyone,
but she was the only one who truly understood, who
truly appreciated.

All questions were answered in the night, all problems
ceased to exist for a little while.

III.

It was strange, and sad, how a child could know all this—
about insignificance and beauty and peace

While other people might go their whole lives without
noticing anything at all.

Over time, they came to understand and appreciate the
stars a little more, but only because of the child.

The child was said, by the legends, to have been
the star child.

The pensive side of me.

Stars are my favourite things in the whole world. I know it sounds cheesy but it's true. On summer nights, I will sometimes go outside and lie on my deck just looking at the sky. Or if I'm flying on a plane late at night, I will stargaze out the window the entire flight.

The line "They were a sign that something beautiful could light up the darkness" was inspired by a flight home from L.A. to Pittsburgh. I was listening to the song "Outro" by M83 and thinking about how dark and endless the night seemed, yet how beautiful and bright the stars were. I wrote the line down in my journal and went to sleep, and when I woke up, I wrote the poem.

CHAPTER 11

The Need to Compete

Me doing ta-da arms in New York City, in the summer of 2009, just before I won my first national title at the Dance Educators of America competition for my musical theater solo, "I Like to Fuss."

*H*ave you ever seen that Thanksgiving episode of *Friends* where the Geller siblings, Monica and Ross, play football with the gang? And it turns out their parents refused to let them play football after Monica broke Ross's nose during their family's annual Thanksgiving game because she was sooo competitive?

Yeah, I'm that girl.

When I was little, I was a normal amount of competitive but not *super* competitive. I became that way when I joined *Dance Moms*, I think. I mean, not only were we competing against other teams in local, regional and national tournaments, but we were also competing against each other weekly to be at the top of the pyramid.

The thing is, I think it's *great* to be super competitive. My parents raised me that way, and *they* are that way; we are truly a family of Monicas. I know that in Gram's gener-ation, and to some extent in my mom's, too, girls weren't supposed to want to win, win, win; it wasn't considered a feminine trait. But among my generation, anyway, competitiveness has no gender. No mat-ter how we self-identify, we are free to be competitive—and to be proud of our inner Monicas, too!

That being said, those gender stereo-types *can* sneak in. One day on the set of the movie *A Cowgirl's Story* (more on that later!), a spontaneous football game just kind of happened. We were filming at a high school, so we had a whole sports field at our disposal, and one of the guys, my friend Aedin Mincks, had brought a football to the set.

After that first national dance title, I went out for celebration ice cream at Ellen's Stardust Diner in NYC with my friends from the studio.

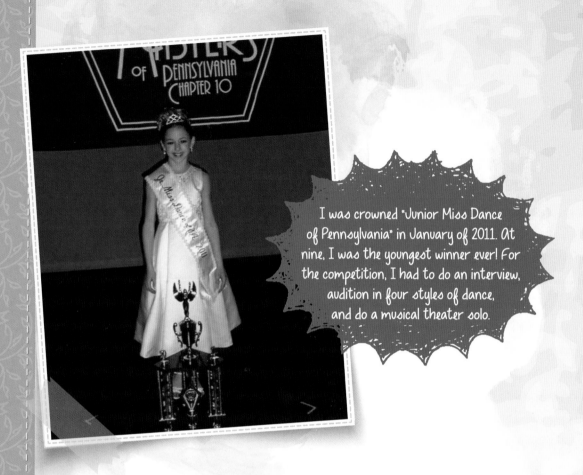

I was crowned "Junior Miss Dance of Pennsylvania" in January of 2011. At nine, I was the youngest winner ever! For the competition, I had to do an interview, audition in four styles of dance, and do a musical theater solo.

So there we were, Aedin and I and a bunch of the extras, playing in the wet grass. I was wearing flip-flops, daisy-print shorts and a black Urban Outfitters T-shirt that said "Sometimes L.A, Sometimes N.Y", and I'd pulled up my hair into my "game on!" ponytail.

At one point I had the ball, and Aedin, who was on the other team, rushed at me and tried to tackle me. He slid into me full force and knocked me off balance, and my feet went up in the air. I heard people gasping and screaming, "NOOOO!"—you know, because Aedin had slammed into the "fragile girl". (Or maybe it was because if anything happened to me, it would mess up the filming schedule, LOL!)

I was fine, and the game continued. I swear, it was just about the most fun I'd ever had. I *loved* scoring touchdowns. I *loved* kicking everyone's butt. Seriously, I would have played all day!

Of course, the competition element on *Dance Moms* was more complicated than in a spontaneous game of football. For one thing, we were all friends, and at the same time, we were all competing against one another. If one of my teammates got first place for her ballet solo, that meant I didn't get first place for *my* ballet solo, and vice versa.

I remember people saying that the show was built on this great rivalry between Maddie Ziegler and me. Yes, she was my biggest rival on the team, I suppose, but she was also one of my best friends. We pushed each other, but in a good way.

Maddie and I also shared one brain, dance-wise. We used to do a lot of duets, and we got to the point where we could literally vibe off each other—like, if we were in the middle of our number and suddenly saw that our steps weren't going to work for the space, we could spontaneously change our choreography with a mere glance or facial

TRUE STORY

This past winter I went ice-skating with a big group of my friends. We kind of split off since there were so many of us, and at one point I decided to skate by myself for a while. So there I was, skating along and minding my own business, when this man passed me on his way to the edge of the rink. He was skating sideways, and just as he passed me he lost his balance and grabbed onto me. This caused me to spin like three or four times, and then I tripped over him and fell flat on my stomach. And guess what? He didn't even fall! He recovered his balance and kept skating to the side of the rink like nothing had happened. I just lay there on my stomach, drenched in icy cold, while all the other skaters skated around me.
Lame.

OKAY, I ADMIT IT, I'M CLUMSY

I'm never going to win any prizes for my gracefulness because I am the clumsiest person in the whole entire world—which is really ironic since I dance. Seriously, I fall or trip at least once every day.

Me and Kendall on the bus on our way to a competition. It's Christmastime—can you tell?

expression or quietly spoken word. It was magical and mysterious.

For example . . . Maddie and I were doing a duet at a shopping centre once, and the stage there turned out to be really small. We hadn't had time for a run-through, and we'd already started our performance, in front of a big audience, when we realized that the stage wasn't large enough for both of us to do our side aerials.

So a couple of counts before the side aerials, when Maddie and I had our backs to the audience, I whispered, "Grand jeté!" Two counts later, she and I did grand jetés instead of the side aerials and then continued seamlessly with the rest of the choreography. No one ever knew. We were so in sync. One brain.

Dance Moms definitely brought out and built up my competitive side. I wanted to win. *We all* wanted to win. But that desire to win wasn't at one another's expense. If one of my teammates won and I didn't, I was disappointed but also genuinely glad for her. I also came to think of my losses as opportunities to grow as a dancer, which has been an important life lesson for me.

Waiting for the awards ceremony during *Dance Moms* Season Seven.

And honestly? During dance competitions, everyone is so focused on winning that no one is called out for being competitive. We're *all* competitive, and that's exactly how it should be.

OK, I have to stop writing now so I can go kick my sister's butt in a game of Skip-Bo.

GAME ON!

In addition to dance (and football!), I enjoy competing at board, card and outdoor games. Some of my favourites (besides Skip-Bo and Phase 10) are Clue, Candy Land, Life, Twister, Cornhole, Red Rover and Freeze Tag.

CHAPTER 12

The Right Shoes

Still trying to figure out the right shoes for these feet.

"**G**ive a girl the right pair of shoes and she can conquer the world."

Yessss.

This quote has a couple of different meanings for me personally. It's even painted on my bedroom wall! I always thought the actor Marilyn Monroe said it, but people say that it was actually the singer Bette Midler and she said it differently. Whoever said it in whatever way, the point is the same. First, a great pair of shoes (whether we're talking high heels or sneakers, Louboutins or Nikes) can make you feel really awesome and self-confident. But more than that, finding the "right shoes" means finding *the thing* that will help you be the best you can be and is the perfect fit *for you*. It may be a pair of pointe shoes or tap shoes. Or a paintbrush. Or a basketball. Or an electron microscope. Or a video camera. Or a surfboard. The possibilities are endless.

Hmm, these shoes aren't bad!

Honestly, though? I'm still trying to figure out the "right shoes" for *me*. I love dancing. I love my new acting career. I'm also starting to get into clothing design.

But I'm a teenager. I change my mind a lot. Part of it is that I can imagine so many other things I could do when I grow up. My dad has often said I'd make a good lawyer because I'm great at arguing (ha!). I can also see myself as a doctor, maybe a general surgeon like one of my favourite TV heroes, Meredith on *Grey's Anatomy*. And of course, I'd love to write more books because, well, books are the ultimate, plus I am having SO MUCH FUN writing this one and sharing all my stories with you guys!

Still, when I contemplate any of these possible futures, my brain goes into worrying and overthinking mode (of course): "I could try to make it as an actor, but what if I fail at that? . . . And what if I fail at dancing, too? . . . I can't be a lawyer because I'd have to make straight As in high school and college to get into law school, and how can I make straight As while I'm dancing AND pursuing my acting career AND all the zillions of other things I have going on? . . . And I can't be a doctor because of the straight As business, plus I hate science plus SEVEN YEARS OF MEDICAL SCHOOL AND RESIDENCY TRAINING . . . and . . . and . . . and . . ."

I will always feel at home in these shoes.

You get the picture.

Sometimes it's hard for me to hold steady with all this pressure and confusion. There are days when I fly home from a gruelling week of dance rehearsals and filming and movie auditions in Los Angeles and I think, "I can't do this anymore. What if I'm putting myself under all this stress and none of it works out?" Days like that, I just want to curl up in bed and stay there for the rest of my life.

But there are other days when I jump out of bed full of energy and excitement and optimism, and I'm like, "Today I'm going to tackle a tonne of homework and take a couple of dance classes and pack for my L.A. trip. I can be whatever I want someday . . . a doctor or lawyer or dancer or actor . . . or a doctor who dances, or a lawyer who acts on the side . . . or a full-time author . . . or a designer of super-cool, super-comfy dance gear . . . or some wonderful profession I haven't even thought of yet . . ."

So basically, on any given day, I'm somewhere on the continuum between hiding in bed and conquering the universe. Luckily, there's almost always something that inspires me to get up if I happen to be in Hiding in Bed mode. It might be a big thing, like an important meeting with an agent or the first day filming a new movie. Or it might be a small thing, like a book I really, really want to read or my dad waking me up for my online Chemistry exam. (I also have some "Get your butt out of bed, Chloe!" strategies that I will share with you later.)

And my dad? When I have one of my worrying, overanalyzing, "What am I going to do with my life?" freak-outs, he is the one who talks me down and reminds me that as long as I take my schoolwork seriously, I will always have the option of going to college when I'm eighteen, which means that I don't have to make those all-important decisions about my future *right this second*.

(Although we recently talked about how I *could* finish up my

WELCOME TO MY HOMESCHOOL!

In case you're wondering what homeschooling is like, here is an overview of my programme and my day-to-day. Everyone does it differently, though; homeschooling can be individually tailored to a student's needs. Also, each state has different laws and requirements regarding what, when, how and how much homeschoolers have to do. (I homeschool according to Pennsylvania laws.)

* I homeschool through a cyberschool. My subjects are divided into four quarters, and I have two months to complete each quarter. This means that I can set my own pace over those two months in terms of how (and how quickly) to finish all my work.

* Typically, my daily "class" on any given subject consists of me reading a bunch of pages on the topic and taking a five-question quiz afterwards. I also watch short videos and do other activities, too. After every five lessons (so normally Fridays, if I'm on track!), I have a nineteen-question quiz that consists of fifteen multiple-choice and four written-response questions.

* The cyberschool programme has teachers I can always contact and speak to, just like regular teachers. I also have access to video lectures and websites related to what I'm studying.

* This year, I'm taking: English, Spanish, Algebra 2, US Politics, Anatomy, Chemistry, Health and Creative Writing (my favourite!).

* With the science classes, I actually do "practicals" but they're really more like online activities that simulate lab work (like it will say: "Imagine that you have a vial of water and you fill it with salt … what would the salt do?").

* With my creative writing assignments, I'll usually do an outline (unless it's a poem), first draft, second draft, third draft and final draft.

✻ Self-management wasn't always a strong skill of mine, so when I first started homeschooling, I had a hard time with *not* having classes and homework every day like in regular school. Having two months to complete a class makes it easy to procrastinate . . . "I'll just take this week off and do double next week." I've got a little better about it, though.

✻ If I do fall behind, the cyberschool people will contact my mom and dad and say, "Chloe's a little behind—she needs to catch up." And I do fall behind—these days, not so much because of procrastination but because my schedule is so crazy busy. It's especially hard when I'm in L.A. and I have a bunch of auditions plus dance.

✻ Do I have a straight-A average? Not at the moment, although my grades are pretty good.

✻ Do I miss regular school? Just the social aspect of it and also getting out of the house, LOL. I don't miss stuff like PE and lunch, which I feel make everyone's day unnecessarily long.

Sometimes, of course, I need a study break.

WHICH CHLOE

AM I TODAY?

Confession: I go through these phases where I try out a different style every few days. For a few days it might be boho, then super girlie, then all black. It's like I'm trying out different versions of me to see what fits.

I also try out different versions of the *inner* me to see what fits. Do I want to be known for being nice? Or do I want to be known for my clever sarcasm? My personality has all these aspects to it, and I can't decide if I want to be Nice Chloe or Sarcastic Chloe or some other Chloe.

Decisions, decisions . . .

schooling when I'm seventeen and start college then. Eek!)

I'm fortunate to have the family I have. They love me unconditionally and support me fiercely and help me plan for my future. Still, ultimately it's up to me and me alone to decide who I am. Not my family or my friends or my teachers or the world at large. *Me.*

I had this insight about myself the other day that made me feel very grown up and wise. It was inspired by what my dad said about keeping my options open for the future. I realized that even though I'm taking acting classes and going to auditions and appearing in movies *in the present*, it doesn't mean I'm absolutely, definitely, one hundred percent committed to an acting career *in the future*. Same with, say, if I choose to intern at a law office or sign up for a creative writing course or take a pre-med course at a local university. It's the journey that matters, not the destination. That's part of what I meant when I said that everything happens for a reason. Maybe I'll intern at a law office next summer . . . and what if they happen to have a branch in Paris, which will inspire me to study French online, which will lead me to do a semester abroad in Provence, which will make me want to become a French teacher? Or . . . what if I take that pre-med course at the local university, and I walk into the wrong lecture hall and hear an amazing talk about coral reefs, and I end up becoming a marine biologist?

It's not about how the experience can make you better at *that thing*. It's how the experience can change you as a person and take you down new and unexpected paths.

Translation: I may be trying on a *lot* of shoes before I settle on the right pair. Which is just fine with me!

Short Story

by Chloe Lukasiak

This is a short story I wrote for my creative writing class. It's entirely fictional and not based on anyone you know. Really.

My life is boring. Yes, I know everyone says that, but my life really is boring. I get up every day at 6:30 a.m. and go to school. I normally do my hair and make-up the same every single day—straight hair with a little make-up, not much, but enough that I look like I'm alive. I always end up wearing jeans and some kind of boring shirt. See? Pretty boring.

Wait—it gets better. So I go to my homeroom with the same boring people. Everyone's either sleeping or copying Leo's homework. Leo is the smart one in our class; you know, the kid who is so naturally super smart that you just wonder how much easier life would be if you were as naturally super smart as him. We all know that kid. Well, yeah, Leo is that kid in our homeroom.

Then I go to Algebra 2. I hate algebra. I'm actually really good at algebra, but I just hate it. There is nothing exciting or creative or new about it. You walk into algebra class every day and what do you learn? You learn about a bunch of letters and symbols that represent numbers or whatever and then you have to add, subtract, multiply or divide based on *more* symbols. Boring.

After putting up with *that* bit of insufferable, I go to English. Now, English is my favourite. I love reading and writing more than just about anything. If someone came up to me tomorrow and told me that I could only do reading and writing for the rest of my life, I would probably be the happiest person in the whole world.

Actually . . . I wouldn't mind it if that person told me I had to travel, too. I would love travelling, I bet. I wouldn't know because I've never left this small, depressing town. Seeing different places every week, experiencing different cultures . . . now, *that*? That's LIVING.

Although I guess I travel to new places when I read. I travel to the worlds that exist inside the stories. I love being so caught up in a book that I forget that I'm not actually, literally living in that world. That? That's one of the few non-boring parts of my life.

OK. So I could sit here and tell you about the rest of my school day, but it's pretty boring and, well, school sucks. That's all there is to it. So after school, my mom picks me up and we have the same conversation every single day. You know—how was whatever? *Boring* . . .

I go home, I start my homework, and I normally get something to eat. I could lie to you that I snack on something healthy like an apple or a granola bar. But I don't. I normally snack on some chocolate or microwaved mac and cheese or fries. I know you do, too, so don't bother lying. We all do it.

Then I go to dance. Yes, I'm a dancer. I love dance. Dance is like the only major non-boring part of my day besides English class and reading books. Dance class usually goes on all night and I normally have it every day of the week except for Tuesdays and Fridays. I come home after, get dinner, take a shower, finish my homework, all that super-boring stuff. My absolute, absolute favourite part of the day is when I finally get to lie in bed and read. That's the best. I love reading. I know you do, too; otherwise, you wouldn't have read this story. Or maybe you had to? Well, if you did, that's boring. I'm sorry.

Maybe it'll all get better. Maybe one day I'll disappear into my stories forever and then life won't be so boring. You know?

Ever since I left public school to be homeschooled, I've struggled with whether or not I should go back. Being the overthinker and worrier that I am, I'm often weighing the pros and cons and trying to make a decision. Right. This. Second.

This short story kind of became all the cons of public school mashed together. Like how I used to have to wake up really, really early every morning. Like how badly I wanted to fit in. Like how a lot of the students seemed to wear the same outfit—jeans and a sweater and sneakers—so I wore it, too. There is nothing wrong with this outfit at all. But the reason I wore it every day was because I wanted to be like everyone else and not myself.

CHAPTER 13

Doing Scary Stuff

✿ (aka ADVENTURES IN ACTING) ✿

My first movie! I'm holding my copy of the DVD! Yay!

*I*n September 2015, I received a call that would change everything. I had got a part in a movie that I had auditioned for, called *Center Stage: On Pointe*.

But let me back up a bit and explain to you how I went from *Dance Moms* to Hollywood.

One day, sometime after leaving *Dance Moms*, I told my parents that I thought I might want to try acting, maybe take an acting class. Acting had always been a dream of mine—inspired, in part, by my passion for reading. I love, love, love novels, but I can't live in those fictional worlds in real life. For me, acting seemed like a wonderful way to live in made-up worlds.

Fortunately, my parents didn't raise their eyebrows and say: "Um . . . acting? Really, honey?" They totally, one hundred percent supported me. My mom found us a little apartment in Los Angeles so we could live there part-time and I could audition for roles.

I won't lie to you—it was scary diving into the unknown. I didn't really have any acting experience, just some scenes from *To Kill a Mockingbird* and a few other plays when I was in sixth grade at my performing arts school.

ADVICE FOR ACTING (AND LIVING)

Another thing I've learned in my acting classes is: bring your own POV (point of view) to a scene. You have to know who you are as a character in every word you speak, every action you perform, or you'll get lost and become overpowered by other actors' and characters' POVs.

This is true in life, too. Always bring your own POV and stand behind it; don't let other people take over who you are or what you're thinking or feeling. With every role, whether real or made-up, you have to bring yourself into it.

On the set of *A Cowgirl's Story*—the school cafeteria. I was running through my lines in my head before they called "Action!"

But I made myself be brave. No pain, no gain. Fake it till you make it. First, I signed up for acting classes. I took technique classes, how-to-audition classes, comedy classes and drama classes. I got so much out of all of them (and I continue to take lessons whenever I can).

And while I was learning, I started going out for auditions. At one point—maybe after a dozen or so auditions?—I sent in a self-taped audition (these are getting pretty common in the industry) for one of the lead roles in the movie *Center Stage: On Pointe*.

And then I got The Call. It turned out I was too young to play any of the roles in the movie. But they had liked my audition tape so much that they decided to create a whole new part for me, which I thought was the coolest thing ever. I was going to be Gwen, a young ballet protégé who has to keep up with the older kids at a dance camp. Honestly, it was THE perfect role for me.

(It's all a blur now, but after I hung up, I might have done a crazy-happy dance and screamed, "I'M GOING TO BE IN A MOVIE!" at the top of my lungs. Sorry, neighbours!)

In October, I had to report to the set in Vancouver. Mom came with me, of course. There was a week of rehearsal before we started filming. It was a pretty intense schedule. We filmed for about four weeks, and it was rainy the whole time. (Now I know why people call Vancouver "Raincouver"! Not that I minded . . . Rainy days are my favourite.)

It was National Kissing Day (yes, that's a thing!), so I decided to kiss one of the beautiful animals at the ranch where we were filming A Cowgirl's Story.

PREPARING
FOR A ROLE

Before I have to do a scene (whether for an audition, a read-through, a rehearsal or the cameras), I like to go through the script and make lots and lots of notes.

I will write down what my character is feeling at various points in the script, like: "I'm disappointed here." "I'm curious but I don't want to show it." "I'm relieved." "I'm sooo excited!" It's all about the journey of becoming someone else and processing the world through that person's lens. (I also love being able to express emotion in a role because I'm very emotional in my dancing.)

I will also go through the script and write down what time of day it is, where I am, what the weather's like, and so forth. It helps me to say my lines more meaningfully if I know that my character is huddled under a bus shelter during a chilly downpour versus, say, taking a walk on a warm spring day.

Another useful thing I learned in one of my acting classes is using my own emotions or state of mind. If I'm tired from the previous night, I can use it for my character. I can think: "Why is my character tired here? Did she stay up super late with her friends? Is she pulling Hermione Granger hours at the library because she's determined to get straight As? Is she coming down with a cold?" These kinds of questions allow me to create a deeper, more nuanced character.

Because this was my first movie role, I was SO NERVOUS. But it was a great set for a newbie like me, a great intro to the film world in general, because everyone was so sweet *and* fun *and* really professional. I was the youngest cast member—fourteen—but the others really made me feel at home, especially Maude Green, who was seventeen and the closest to me age-wise.

Bailee Madison and me between takes. This was one of the first days of filming *A Cowgirl's Story.*

The director, Director X, was super chill and nice. *And* talented—in addition to films, he's done a tonne of cool music videos for singers like Drake, Jay-Z, Usher, Kanye West and others. I learned a lot seeing everything through his directorial eye, which was different from what I was used to artistically. It was pretty exciting for me and planted another seed in my head, like maybe I'd enjoy being a director someday?

Since *Center Stage*, I've got roles in two other movies: *A Cowgirl's Story* (directed by Timothy Armstrong) and *Loophole* (directed by Jenni Ivers). I've also done a short film, *Beautiful Scars* (directed by Paul D. Hannah). Each project has taught me new skills about being a better actor (and a better person). And all of my characters have been *so* different!

I'm also continuing to audition for more roles . . .

. . . aaand I'm continuing to pile up the rejections, too. I mean, I'm so, so grateful for the successes I've had, but I won't lie to you—the

This is the outfit I wore for our equestrian drill team competitions in *A Cowgirl's Story*.

Shooting *Beautiful Scars*.

At the premiere of *A Cowgirl's Story* with *Dance Moms* executive producer Bryan Stinson.

rejections are *hard*. In the beginning, I was heartbroken after every "no". I cried and cried, thinking: "What am I doing? I'm not an actor. I'll never be an actor. This is stupid. I'm wasting my time and my mom's time and everyone else's time . . ."

But I didn't give up. I pushed through it. As a result, each rejection got a little easier to bear; I would try to learn from the experience and do even better at my next audition. I definitely became a stronger person.

Acting has helped me in other ways, too. I *may* have mentioned earlier that I'm kind of a shy person. Acting has made me more outgoing. Another way to put it—and I hope this makes sense!—is that acting has helped me to be myself.

Oh, and did I mention my singing? I've always liked to sing in the shower, but that was about the extent of my vocal abilities. So when I had to sing for a movie audition (I sang "Lost Boy"), my manager and agent were like,

Speaking of scary stuff . . .

So I was afraid of everything until about age ten. Like *everything*. Of course the usual things like spiders, clowns, being alone in dark basements, ghost trains, haunted mazes and roller coasters. Also the animated *Snow White and the Seven Dwarfs* movie. (Please don't laugh at me!)

And then I decided to stop being such a baby and grow some courage. This was the beginning of my Fearless Chloe phase . . .

. . . which lasted until seventh grade when I saw a horror movie called *The Conjuring* with my friends. In case you haven't seen it, it's about a family who is being tormented by demons and ghosts. In a secluded farmhouse. AND IT'S BASED ON A TRUE STORY. I'm pretty sure I was the only one of my friends who was crying through the entire movie. (Oh, and . . . did I mention that the family's youngest daughter had long, curly blonde hair and brown eyes? That wasn't creepy AT ALL . . .)

I still have nightmares about that movie.

Now I hate anything to do with demons and dark spirits, and if anyone brings them up, I just completely lose my calm. I don't mess with that kind of stuff, and I don't take the subject lightly.

P.S. *But* my biggest fear is probably when I'm home alone and I sneeze and someone says, "Bless you." I mean, how can you not be scared of that? Didn't I tell you my house is haunted?

PLAYING THE BAD GUY

People have asked me if I would ever play a character I didn't like, as in, would I ever play a criminal? A bully? My answer is yes! That's what acting is all about. Even if you can't personally relate to the character, you have to think about her actions and her attitudes from *her* perspective. You can't hate your character, no matter what. Also, if you dig deep enough, you'll find out why she is the way she is. You might find some piece of her that's relatable to you, too, like: when your character was little, she had a dog she loved, and so did you.

This is a jail from the set of the movie *Suicide Squad*.

"Um . . . maybe you should take a few lessons?" They were right! I hadn't exactly done justice to Ruth B.'s song . . . not even close.

I started studying with a vocal teacher named Evelyn, who has a studio in the basement of her house. I have a lesson with her whenever I have to sing for an audition.

(By the way, generally after an audition, I like to review the video and watch the scene; it really helps me with my acting. I haven't got to the point where I can listen to myself singing, though. Soon. Maybe. Someday.)

For so many years, dancing was second nature to me, as natural as breathing. Now I'm learning how to be an actor. I'm also learning how to sing. And who knows what's next? Maybe directing, producing, writing scripts . . .

It's hard being a beginner again, but it's exhilarating, too. I'm growing and exploring new dreams; I'm developing new muscles.

I'm learning archery for a new movie called *The Message*, directed by Timothy Armstrong (who also directed *A Cowgirl's Story*).

CHAPTER 14

Dance Moms:
✷ PART 2 ✷

Getting ready to surprise everyone at the *Dance Moms Season Seven* finale.

One night in December 2016, I walked into my parents' room to ask my mom something. She was in there alone, sitting on the bed with a strange expression on her face, so I was like, "What's up?"

She told me that she'd just heard some news about *Dance Moms*. She wasn't one hundred percent sure, but she thought they might be filming their series finale soon.

Series finale, not *season* finale.

I didn't know how to react to this. I mean, I knew the show would end *someday*. But hearing it stated like this made it very real for me.

This news churned up so many emotions. Yes, my mom and I left the show a long time ago, and for good reason. It just wasn't the right place for us anymore. But *Dance Moms* was my childhood—*literally* my childhood, because when I think back on being a kid, I think: *Dance Moms*. Those girls were my sisters. I spent every waking hour with them, practically.

A chapter in my life was ending. It had technically already ended in 2014; still, I'd always figured in the back of my mind that I could go back someday and maybe make a guest appearance, say hi to my old friends.

Me, Kendall, Camryn Bridges, Kalani Hilliker, and Nia—together again!

But this . . . this was forever. A door was about to slam shut in my face and never open again.

Tears filled my eyes. My mom hugged me and hugged me. Then, after the shock had subsided, a crazy idea came to me.

"What if I went on the series finale to say goodbye?"

"That's funny, Chlo."

"No, I'm serious, Mom."

Well, one thing led to another. Mom got in touch with the show's producers, and after that conversation we were officially invited to guest-appear on the finale, which would take place before and during Nationals in New Jersey.

Gulp!

Part of me was really excited. The other part of me was like, "Is it too late to change my mind?" I started second-guessing myself. How would the girls react when I showed up? How would my old coach react?

The day Mom and I drove to New Jersey to film, I managed to keep my emotions under control. In the car, I sang the song "Car Radio" by the band twenty one pilots, over and over again, a cappella (i.e., no instruments to drown out my sorry voice). I had begun memorizing the lyrics earlier because my friend had bet me that I couldn't do so in less than two days, and obviously I had to prove her wrong! After my twelfth take, my mom was like, "Can't you sing something else?" But I was determined to get to the end of the song and nail every single lyric. (Which I did, and I was super proud of myself, because I am the biggest dork in the universe.)

Mom and I were making *surprise* guest appearances; none of the girls or moms knew we would be there. When I walked onto the set (aka the dressing room), everybody freaked out. I said the first thing that popped into my head, which was, "Who missed me?" When Nia realized it was us, she leaped out of her chair, slipped and fell, then got right back up and sprinted toward me. We ran toward each other, laughing and crying, and hugged for about a million years. I was so happy to see her and Kendall and Kalani and the other girls, and the moms, too.

The day went better than I could have ever hoped for. The girls and I did our Eight-Count Ritual together (see below!). I gave them a pep talk for Nationals.

THE EIGHT-COUNT RITUAL

I learned this exercise in dance class when I was seven, and I still do it to warm up and to shake out my nerves before rehearsals, auditions, competitions and other occasions when I have to be "on". Now that I'm dancing competitively again, the girls and I do it together before every performance.

(And if I ever become a surgeon, I'll probably do it before every operation!)

Backstage with Nia.

- Shake your right hand eight times.
- Shake your left hand eight times.
- Shake your right foot eight times.
- Shake your left foot eight times.
- Repeat steps 1-4 four times each.
- Repeat steps 1-4 two times each.
- End by shaking your whole body.

Now you're ready to go!

This was a *huge* change for me from 2014. Back then, the adults were the ones to give us pep talks. I just listened along with the rest of the girls.

Now *I* was doing the talking. I had definitely grown up; I had my own voice now, my own things to say. I then gave a *second* pep talk, this time to my mom, which was even more of a role reversal. (Of course Mom teared up; I wasn't that little girl anymore.)

Maybe the most important thing to come out of the day, though, was my big "aha" moment, my announcement.

"I've been thinking about competing again," I told everyone.

New team jackets!

PRE-PERFORMANCE
JITTERS

Speaking of things staying the same...

So the older, wiser, stronger me still gets major jitters before competitions, especially on camera. When I went back to the show and competed on camera for the first time in a while, I was sooo nervous.

What am I like when I'm freaking out pre-performance? My heart races, and my stomach feels like it's trying to push its way out of my body. I start shaking and sort of hyperventilating. I want to throw up.

How do I deal with it? Well, I take a lot of deep breaths. I stretch. I listen to music. I do the Eight-Count Ritual, either alone or with my team. I tell myself that I know how to do this . . . that I'm capable of learning a new dance on Tuesday, rehearsing it on Wednesday, Thursday and Friday, and nailing it in front of the judges on Saturday.

(OK, and this may sound weird, but . . . sometimes, I try to make myself freak out when I'm alone in my room, and bring on all those awful physical symptoms, just so I can practise how to ignore them, get rid of them or solve the problem another way. Yup. I do that.)

As soon as I said those words out loud, I was sure. I *did* want to compete again—but this time on my own terms. I had taken the year off from the competition circuit, and I was ready to jump back in.

Well, even before filming was over, the producers wanted to have another conversation with Mom and me. They explained that they had

Backstage with the girls! (From left to right: Nia, Kendall, me, Kalani, and Camryn.)

decided it wasn't going to be the series finale of the show after all and asked if we would like to come back for more episodes.

I laughed (in a nervous, *ohmigosh!* way) when I heard this. I'd felt really good about making one last appearance to say goodbye to my friends, my childhood. But going *back* back was a whole other thing.

Mom and I had more family meetings and talks, and in the end, we decided yes. I was at a different place in my life than when we'd left the first time around. I wanted to take a chance on *Dance Moms* as the older, wiser, stronger Chloe—not the scared, anxious, timid Chloe I used to be. I was in control of my choices.

Things happened very quickly after that. Mom and I flew out to Los Angeles to film me dancing for Murrieta Dance Project, which is based in Murrieta, California, and headed up by Erin Babbs. This meant competing against my friends, which was so weird—but Erin is an awesome coach.

Then out of the blue, at the end of March, my old coach announced on social media she was leaving the show, and Cheryl Burke filled in for her—the amazing, unbelievably talented Cheryl Burke.

So I've been training under Cheryl along with Nia, Kendall, Kalani and Camryn. Our team name is the Irreplaceables. Can I tell you how much I love being back? And how much I love being coached by Cheryl, who is so nice and down-to-earth and also a brilliant coach? She pushes us, but only in the most positive ways. She doesn't try to force us to be "perfect"; she just wants us to be the best we can be.

Everything happens for a reason. Somehow, my choices—*my* choices—led me on a path back to *Dance Moms*.

I'm embracing the journey, guys.

Last day of rehearsals with Nia, Kendall, me, Kalani, Cheryl Burke, Camryn, and dancer/choreographer Ryan Ramirez

MUSCLE MEMORY

Muscle memory is this cool thing where, if you repeat an activity enough times, your motor system will basically store the memory of how to perform that activity and make it easier for you to perform it in the future—in other words, you will be able to do it without thinking about it much. It's like riding a bicycle; once your body has that skill down, you can go bike riding without much conscious effort on your part (like "I have to put my feet here . . . and push against the pedals over and over again if I want to move forward . . . right foot, left foot, right foot . . .").

Dancers count on muscle memory for performances. If you practise a dance enough times and for long enough, you should be able to do it without having to run through it step-by-step in your head: "OK, now I have to relevé with my arms in fifth . . . then run to the left and jeté . . . then . . ." The problem with *Dance Moms* is, we always learn our competition dances three or four days before the competition. It's always been that way. So we can't rely on muscle memory to help us out. Which can make remembering and executing the dances a *lot* more difficult.

In case you were wondering . . .

Backstage at the rehearsal for our dance number "The Coven." That's Nia and Camryn in the foreground and Cheryl Burke in the background.

My POV when I do *Dance Moms* on-set interviews. Here are executive producer Bryan Stinson and members of the crew.

WATCHING DANCE MOMS

I mentioned earlier that after the first few episodes of Season One, I stopped watching for a bunch of reasons, although I always liked checking out our old dance routines on YouTube. I did watch full episodes once in a while, though. And whenever I did, it was such an interesting disconnect between who I was in the episode and who I was in the present. Of course I was aware of myself growing up—we're all aware of ourselves growing up—but watching the process unfold on TV was sooo strange!

(BTW, I *did* watch the full episode where I returned. I wanted to see if they showed Nia falling as she ran toward me. They did!)

CHAPTER 15

My Unglamorous Glamorous Life

Yeah, no biggie. Just hanging out with Michael Douglas (!!!) at the International Day of Peace event at the United Nations in New York City. Maddi Jane is on the left. The guy on the far right is Crawford Collins; next to him is Chris Collins.

$\mathcal{M}$y life is non-stop red carpets and photo shoots and celebrity-filled parties.

Not.

My typical day is filled with school, dance classes, rehearsals, more school and more dance. And sometimes auditions. And sometimes acting workshops and singing lessons. The bottom line is, I work really, really hard.

I don't mean to downplay or diminish what I have. I know I have kind of a cool career (or careers, plural), and that I'm incredibly fortunate to have had so many opportunities. My time on *Dance Moms* from 2011 to 2014 was challenging, but it was also *amazing*. I got to dance, which was and is my number one passion; I got to be on TV; I got to travel; and I got to be with my best friends pretty much constantly.

Now, as I write this, I'm back on *Dance Moms*, and it's awesome. I love my teammates (including the girls I danced with before), I love our new coach, Cheryl, and I love competing again. I'm also pursuing my acting classes and going on lots of auditions.

And I won't lie . . . I *do* go to fancy events once in a while, especially

MY FIRST JOB

When I was little, Gram would give me five dollars and I would clean her dining-room mirrors, which were full-length. I considered this to be my "work" (and honestly, five dollars is a lot of money for a kid!). I loved going to her house to do my job; also, she kept a big bowl of Hershey's Kisses around, which was an extra incentive for me!

MY MOVIE
DORKDOM

I think I mentioned before that if I like a movie that I see in the cinema, I have to go back and see it a second time (or sometimes even a third time). I saw *Miss Peregrine's Home for Peculiar Children* twice. I saw *The Martian* twice. I saw *Nerve* twice. If my friends invite me to see a movie and I've already seen it, I always struggle with: "Should I tell them I already saw this one and risk having them think I'm weird, or should I keep it to myself and act surprised and scared or whatever during the appropriate moments in the movie?"

Also, you guys need to know this about me: I am a huge *Star Wars* and Marvel geek. Like, HUGE. I've seen every *Star Wars* movie and every Marvel movie many, many times. (Except for the second *Spider-man* with Andrew Garfield because—MASSIVE SPOILER ALERT!!!!! SKIP RIGHT TO THE NEXT PARAGRAPH IF YOU HAVEN'T SEEN IT!!!!!—Gwen Stacy dies. So I can only see the first one.)

I'll totally go to the movies by myself if I have to. After my third eye surgery, the new *Star Wars* movie had just come out, and I really, really, REALLY wanted to see it. So I asked my mom if she could drop me off at the cinema. I think it was like 1:30 p.m. on a Wednesday, and I saw it by myself with my one good eye (the other one was bandaged up), and it was AWESOME.

when I'm in Los Angeles. I'm invited to a lot of movie premieres, which I love because I'm a *huge* movie buff. Even after all this time, though, I still feel awestruck and starry-eyed about these kinds of things, like I'm this regular small-town girl from Pennsylvania, and how did I get to be so lucky? I will never take what I have—these special moments, these opportunities—for granted.

Anyway, so, yes . . . I know that my life is sometimes kinda glamorous. But at the same time, it's really quite unglamorous. Let me explain. Here's a typical day for me in L.A. (i.e., my work-home):

- Wake up whenever jet lag lets me wake up.
- Eat breakfast.
- Do schoolwork.
- Get dressed.
- Normally I have meetings or an audition (this usually takes up the whole day, so I try to fit lunch in there somewhere).
- Sometimes I also have acting classes.
- Go to a dance class or to the gym or maybe for a run.
- Eat dinner.
- Do more schoolwork.
- Catch up on my e-mails, texts, etc.
- Read a book or watch TV.

ME AND MY ASTHMA

Here is an unglamorous fact about me: I've suffered from asthma all my life. Sometimes it really affects me, and other times it doesn't bother me. One day it was raining, and I was rehearsing a group dance, and the asthma was so bad and I was so out of breath that I thought I was going to be sick. The next day, I was fine. It can be unpredictable. Just in case, I have to be sure to always have my inhaler with me and use it when I need it. Having to be vigilant about my health definitely keeps things real for me.

Getting my makeup done before the *Pete's Dragon* premiere.

Sometimes, there will be a special event to attend or a photo shoot. If I'm filming (for *Dance Moms* or for a new movie), the above schedule goes out the window and the filming will take up huge, huge blocks of my day.

And even less glamorous is a typical day for me in Mars (i.e., my home-home):

- Wake up around 8:00 a.m.
- Eat breakfast.
- Get dressed.
- Do lots of schoolwork.
- Eat lunch and either read a book or catch up on things I have to do (like e-mails and texts).
- Finish my schoolwork.
- Go to a dance class.
- Come home, eat dinner.
- Read more or maybe watch TV.

This was a photo shoot for social media.

FANGIRLING

Years ago, all the *Dance Moms* girls were walking the red carpet—it was one of the early Teen Choice Awards ceremonies. We were SO EXCITED to be part of such a glamorous event. At one point we decided to go up to every famous person who was there and ask to get a picture with them—Selena Gomez, Justin Bieber, Ariana Grande and a bunch of others. We were that group of annoying kids running around with our phones and begging for photos with anyone who was a celebrity or who looked like they might be a celebrity.

I don't do this anymore, although if I ever met Cate Blanchett, I would definitely beg her for a picture—she's my acting idol!

Clara and I were so excited to meet Bryce Dallas Howard at a private screening of the movie *Pete's Dragon.*

Sometimes, I may have other things to do during the day, too, like filming a YouTube video or taking a yoga class. But other than that, my day-to-day in Mars is pretty routine—mostly schoolwork and dance.

When I'm home, I also have chores. (My mom is rolling her eyes as I write this.) I make my bed every morning (now she's laughing . . . *Mom!*) and I empty the dishwasher. I do my own laundry. I would do more, but my dad likes to be in charge of keeping the house clean, and he's really good at it. He actually *enjoys* vacuuming. Sundays are his cleaning day, and he'll clean the entire house. I pitch in by mopping the kitchen floor, and then afterwards, he and I try to go for a walk around the neighbourhood—it's kind of our thing.

MY FAVORITE TV SHOWS

Some of these I watch for the great acting, some for the stories, some for pure pleasure and some for all of the above!

- Grey's Anatomy
- Friends
- The 100
- Once Upon a Time
- Reign
- Game of Thrones
- Gossip Girl
- Riverdale
- Outlander
- Stranger Things
- The Office
- Vampire Diaries

Marissa Rachel and I are hosting and judging the go90 show Ready! Set! Style.

I'm at the Streamy Awards, which is an awards ceremony for YouTubers and social media influencers.

Jumping in a fountain for photographer Jordan Matter's book *Dancers Among Us.*

Outside our L.A. apartment.

I'm glad that my life is both glamorous and unglamorous. To me, it feels very real, very *me*. I'm lucky, too, because even though I'm still a teenager, I've developed a good work ethic and killer organizational habits. I've *had* to, to accomplish everything I want to accomplish.

I'm not sure what my grown-up future holds. Will I still be dancing? Acting? Will I go to law school or medical school? Will I write a bestselling series about a superhero dancer girl? Whatever path I choose, I know how to work hard. Yes, I mess around sometimes (OK, a *lot*). I sometimes complain about my crazy schedule and threaten to run away to Australia. But it's all good because I'm being true to who I am.

MY FAVORITE MOVIES

✦ The *Pirates of the Caribbean* movies

✦ *Clueless*

✦ Any *Star Wars* movie (including *Episode III: Revenge of the Sith*—don't hate me, fellow *Star Wars* geeks!—because I enjoy watching Anakin's transition)

✦ Any Marvel or DC Comics movie—especially the *Spider-man* movies and *Avengers* movies

✦ *The Hangover*

✦ *The Man from U.N.C.L.E.*

✦ *The Hunger Games* trilogy

✦ *The Breakfast Club*

✦ *Crimson Peak*

✦ *Beauty and the Beast* (the 1991 one and the 2017 one)

CHAPTER 16

Friendships

Hanging out at a Rockette's apartment with my friend Reagan. (The Rockette and Reagan's mom were friends—lucky us!) It was the summer of 2008, and we were in New York City for the Dance Educators of America national competition.

*F*riendships are wonderful. And necessary. And hard. I've been lucky to be blessed with many incredible friends in my life—friends I don't see for years at a time, but then we're able to pick up where we left off like no time has passed; friends who like hanging out and are always up for a movie or shopping or sushi; friends I can call at 4:00 a.m. if I'm having a crisis and can't sleep; friends who will always have my back, no matter what.

Sometimes, though, my insecurity can creep in and make me maybe a little too sensitive and unwilling to trust. I told you guys before that I have a fear of being made fun of. Well, that extends to friends, too. I know it's irrational; my real friends would never, ever make fun of me, at least not intentionally. But having been bullied in the past by people I trusted has left my self-confidence shaky. Like: "Yeah, she says she's my friend, but what did she mean by that comment about my outfit?" Or: "I thought he was cool, so why are he and his friend whispering and pointing at me?"

I'm hoping that once I've made more progress in the self-acceptance department, it will be easier for me to exhale deeply and just enjoy being with my friends without worrying if they're mocking me behind my back.

My twinnie Paige and me just before we take the stage to perform our jazz routine "Chicks Like Us."

But there's a fine line (as I'm sure you know) between a person making a joke and making fun. For me, the red light—the little warning sign in my brain—is if a person (friend or not) says something to me

MEMORIES

At my old house, we had a play set in the back garden, and I used to play on it for hours and hours in the warm weather: swinging, sliding, hanging on the monkey bars. My friends used to play on it with me, too—and one day I decided to make the memories last forever by writing their names on the play set in red paint.

Acting super-goofy with my friend Brittany Pent. (Yes, I'm playing "dead" with a toy sword.)

like, "Where's your sense of humour?" or "Gosh, Chloe, you are SO sensitive!" Then I have to stop, take a beat and assess. Are they right? Am I overreacting? Or were they actually insulting me and are now trying to cover it up by blaming me—like it's my fault, my issue, my thin skin versus their mean, disrespectful behaviour?

It's *complicated.*

The other thing about friends is, it's not easy for me to maintain those relationships when I'm never in one place for very long. *And* working crazy hours. *And* homeschooling. I'm bicoastal between Pennsylvania and California—I mentioned that we have our home-home in Mars and a work-home in L.A.—and I also travel frequently. Some days (and weeks and even months), the only links I have to my friends are by text and Snapchat (or FaceTime if I'm able). Also, not being at the Mars high school, I don't have a chance to hang out with my old friends there or meet new friends.

All this translates into: my closest friends often tend to be "work friends", like other dancers (whether on the current season of *Dance Moms* or at my studio back in Pittsburgh—hi, Anna, Claire, Julia, Madison, Lainy, Izzy, Alexis, Maeve, Brittney and Paige E.!), or other actors (if I'm filming a movie). But then things can shift if I'm not dancing (or acting) with them at the moment. Like what happened after I

Bubble selfie with Paige! I haven't seen her in a while since I've been spending so much time in L.A. But she will always be my twinnie, and whenever we see each other, it's like we never left. Love you, Paige!

BE TRUE

When I was younger, I used to seek the approval of boys more than girls for a very backward reason: I'd been bullied by boys more than girls, and I figured if I could get boys to like me and accept me, they would be nice to me or at least leave me alone. Now that I'm older and wiser (I am almost sixteen, LOL), I know better. My job is not to change who I am, even a tiny bit, to make bullies not bully me. My job is to be true to who I am.

A day off in Disneyland with my *Dance Moms* friends (from left to right: Nia, me, Kalani, Kendall, and Camryn).

left *Dance Moms* in 2014 . . . I was used to seeing those same girls every single day. They were my sisters, and all of a sudden, I wasn't seeing them. I was pretty lonely during that time. It was tough, too, because Mom and I had left the show so abruptly, and so for a while, things were kind of weird between my *Dance Moms* girls and me. When I had my surgery, there were some kind friends who reached out, wished me luck, and sent me Edible Arrangements and other sweet get-well gifts. But for the most part, that was a difficult and lonely period for me, and I'm lucky I had my parents there holding my hand 24/7.

Still, some of my friendships are forever, no matter what happens and no matter where I am. For example, Paige Hyland and I don't see each other as much as we used to, but I will always consider her my

On the set of my friend AJ's music video for his song "Tongue." He was teaching me how to play the piano (just for fun!).

twinnie. She's a forever sister to me, and I don't think that type of friendship ever goes away. Sarah Reasons is one of my closest friends; we met when she joined *Dance Moms* in Season Four.

Also, in general, my friends and I have learned to appreciate whatever time we can spend together. We don't take each other for granted. When I'm back home, we'll be so happy just doing regular boring stuff like going shopping or hanging out at each other's houses and watching silly movies.

And as for dating, well . . . I have some of the same issues with dating that I have with my friendships. I've only had one boyfriend, and it was difficult maintaining a relationship like that when we were both so, so busy and all over the place geography-wise and schedule-wise.

Short Story

by Chloe Lukasiak

This is another short story I wrote for school.

Azalea and Margaret walked along the edge of the pond. The sun was setting, bathing the whole sky in orange and pink, and there was a soft, warm breeze. It was a perfect summer night.

Azalea and Margaret usually talked about anything and everything. They were best friends, and that's what best friends did.

Today, they talked about the upcoming ball. They didn't exactly agree on the subject, though.

"Oh, who needs a ball, anyway?" Margaret scoffed. "It's just a bunch of fools dressed up in stupid frilly gowns and covering their faces with silly masks. I mean, have you ever heard of anything so absurd?" Margaret was the older of the two. She would rather spend her free time reading or learning or exploring nature than going to a frivolous ball.

Azalea was similar to Margaret in that she loved reading and learning. She wasn't sure about the nature part, though. And she was also different from Margaret in that she loved balls, and she loved getting dressed up in silly, frilly gowns. She also loved luncheons and exchanging gossip with the other ladies. Azalea wasn't a gossip, exactly; but she liked finding out the latest news about people they knew so that she and Margaret could laugh about it later—laugh until their stomachs hurt.

Azalea tried to convince her best friend to go to the ball.

"Oh, Margaret! You know how much I love balls. This one will be especially magnificent. The theme is black and white, and I plan to wear a silver gown! My gown is so beautiful, Margaret—really! I tried it on this morning, and you won't believe how the fabric flows and flutters and dances. I truly can't wait to wear it!"

Azalea loved Margaret, but sometimes she wished her friend would enjoy balls and luncheons and gowns and so forth so that she, Azalea, would have someone to share these things with. It was fun for Azalea to meet new people, sure. But Margaret was her best friend.

Margaret seemed to sense this. She grabbed Azalea's hand and looped it through her arm as they walked in the summer night. She thought Azalea's love for balls and luncheons and gowns and so forth was so very silly. But Azalea was her best friend, and whatever made her happy made Margaret happy, too.

To be honest, I have no idea where this story came from. I literally just started writing it one day. Yes, it's about best friends, but I wasn't thinking: "Oh, I want to write a story about best friends who sometimes have different interests." I just kind of started writing, and I liked it, so I kept going.

(This is me trying to be wise and say that sometimes you don't know where life is taking you, but you should just go with it and enjoy the journey. OK, I'll stop being a dork now!)

Sarah and I are at Heinz Field in Pittsburgh. Go, Steelers!

And speaking of friends . . . here I am on the set of *Friends*, one of my favorite TV shows!

I know I'm only a teenager, but I believe in putting my career first. The former First Lady Michelle Obama said in a speech to a group of girls: "There is no boy, at this age, cute enough or interesting enough to stop you from getting your education." Yup! And I feel the same way about my work. I want to be, and become, successful on my own; I want to make that my priority. It wouldn't make sense for who I am to put a boy ahead of my dreams and goals.

(And honestly? I think it would be hard to find someone who understands my schedule and would still want to date me, LOL!)

Anyway · · ·

It's not always easy to be a good friend. I know I'm not perfect; I make mistakes. But I want to be the best friend I can possibly be. I try to be the kind of friend that *I* need. I try to treat my friends the way I would want them to treat me.

I've broken up with friends who couldn't reciprocate. It's never, ever easy to say goodbye to a good friend. But it's more important for me to have people around me who truly love and respect me.

(And, hey . . . if any of my friends are reading this . . . thank you for being there for me, for making me laugh, and for helping me to keep it real!)

CHAPTER 17

Life-Changing Showers

✷ (AND OTHER WAYS TO FIND YOUR CALM) ✷

Some much-needed chill time at the pool.

*L*ike most people, I have big problems and little problems. The thing is, with my overthinking brain, little problems can often spin out of control and morph into big ones.

I guess the point I'm trying to make is, I'm not the most chill, serene, glass-half-full, go-with-the-flow person in the world. Stuff *gets* to me, and then my brain won't let go.

When this happens, and I'm feeling really upset, I often take one of my life-changing showers.

A life-changing shower doesn't *start out* as a life-changing shower. It starts out as a regular, normal, boring, everyday shower, with me singing a "for my ears only" rendition of maybe "Medicine" by Daughter or some M83 song, and being miserable about some problem (which can be anything from "I'm stressed" to "Why did that person say that hurtful thing to me?").

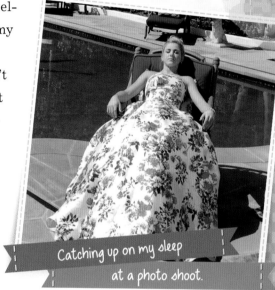
Catching up on my sleep at a photo shoot.

Then at some point, I'll say to myself, "Oh, come on, your life's not so bad. You have SO MUCH to be grateful for." And I will actually begin to feel better.

The other day, I took a life-changing shower and cried about the fact that I was so critical of myself and so sarcastic to others (not funny-sarcastic but kind of mean-sarcastic, which is not cool and which was hurting people's feelings right and left). After a while, I felt very clear-headed. I stopped crying and told myself sternly that I was to *stop* being critical of myself and *stop* being sarcastic to others, end of story.

Outside my studio's dance recital June 2016 in Pittsburgh. This was the first recital I'd skipped ... I was taking the year off from recitals and competitions because I was too busy (and stressed!) and just needed a break. I didn't compete again until my return to *Dance Moms*.

See? It's like instant therapy.

I have other ways of working through my issues, too, like going for a run, taking a long walk, listening to music or catching a yoga or boxing class. (I really like this candlelight yoga class on Tuesday nights near my house because I find candles so relaxing.) There's also a park in my neighbourhood where I like to go if I'm extra stressed or, say, having a fight with my mom (like, I think she's being way overprotective, and she thinks she's just looking out for me . . . typical mom/teenage daughter stuff). I will sit on a bench for a long time, breathe in the fresh air and let myself cool down mentally and emotionally.

I've found, too, that it's harder for me to deal (with life, with problems, with arguments, with anything difficult) when I'm not taking care of myself properly. If I'm living on junk food and not getting enough sleep, for example, my brain is more likely to go into "overload" and lose its ability to cope.

For this reason (and for other reasons, too, like I want to be a healthy person), my goal for this year is to take better care of myself.

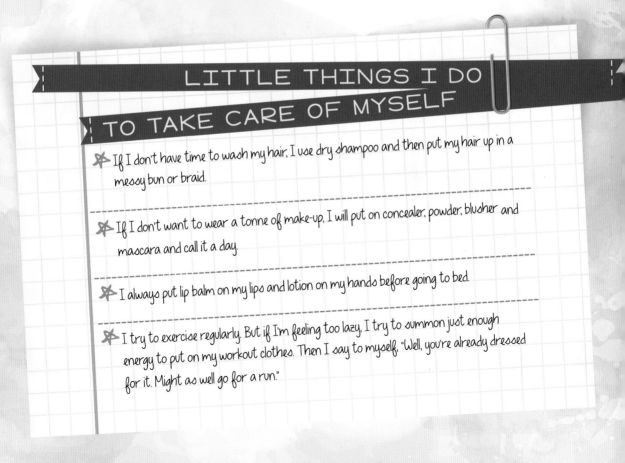

LITTLE THINGS I DO
TO TAKE CARE OF MYSELF

✷ If I don't have time to wash my hair, I use dry shampoo and then put my hair up in a messy bun or braid.

✷ If I don't want to wear a tonne of make-up, I will put on concealer, powder, blusher and mascara and call it a day.

✷ I always put lip balm on my lips and lotion on my hands before going to bed.

✷ I try to exercise regularly. But if I'm feeling too lazy, I try to summon just enough energy to put on my workout clothes. Then I say to myself, "Well, you're already dressed for it. Might as well go for a run."

Here's the plan:

1. Drinking eight cups of water every day. If I'm reading, writing, or studying, I always keep a glass of water next to me. I've also gotten into the habit of drinking a glass of water with every meal and snack, and, of course, during and after dance or jogging or other exercise.

2. Eating healthier. Being homeschooled means having nonstop access to a kitchen (and refrigerator and pantry), and it's just so easy to get up and help myself to a big bowl of Ben & Jerry's Half Baked ice cream whenever I want. (For those of you who've never had this flavor, it's this yummy, amazing combination of chocolate ice cream, vanilla ice cream, fudge brownies, and chocolate chip cookie dough. Oh no, I'm getting a craving . . . Stop it, Chloe!) I try to keep healthy snacks nearby, like baby carrots, apples, oranges, and plain almonds.

3. Getting lots of sleep instead of staying up late with my phone or the TV.

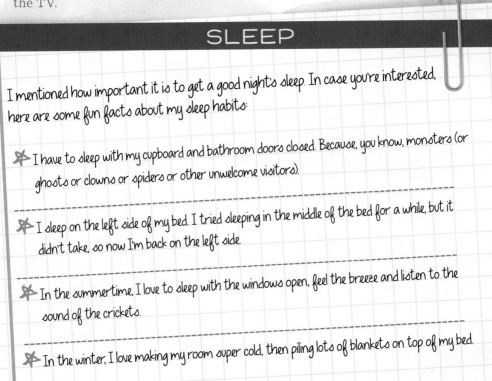

SLEEP

I mentioned how important it is to get a good night's sleep. In case you're interested, here are some fun facts about my sleep habits:

★ I have to sleep with my cupboard and bathroom doors closed. Because, you know, monsters (or ghosts or clowns or spiders or other unwelcome visitors).

★ I sleep on the left side of my bed. I tried sleeping in the middle of the bed for a while, but it didn't take, so now I'm back on the left side.

★ In the summertime, I love to sleep with the windows open, feel the breeze and listen to the sound of the crickets.

★ In the winter, I love making my room super cold, then piling lots of blankets on top of my bed.

4. Getting my work done on time so I'm not stressed out and cramming last-minute.

5. Taking care of my skin, especially my face. I have a new six-step regimen that I try to do every night with these really great products my mom found for me. I wash my face; put on this face-tingling, acne-drying stuff; apply an oil; spray myself with this rosewater mist; then apply a night cream and eye cream. It's way better than what I used to do, which was to fall into bed exhausted with my makeup still on. I still do that sometimes after I've been out with my friends, and I have to have this dialogue with myself: "Come on, get up, wash your face." "Toooo tired." "You're not too tired, you can do it!" "Yeah, no, I can't." When I'm in L.A., though, it's much easier to stick to my nighttime regimen; because of the smog and pollution, I'm really motivated to "wash the day" off my face. During the day, I always, always wear sunscreen, even when it's cold or cloudy.

6. Removing any negative people from my life. By this, I don't mean like if I'm having problems with a friend, that's it, good riddance. Of course we'd work it out. I'm talking about toxic, passive-aggressive, critical, and/or manipulative people who have nothing positive to offer to others.

7. Worrying less about others and more about myself. Or as the saying goes, "Eyes on your own paper." For example . . . I used to get upset when my parents were arguing; I felt like I had to resolve their conflict somehow. But now I know that they'll figure it out themselves because that's what couples do.

Some experts say it takes twenty-one days to form a new habit . . . Others say it's more like months. Whatever the case, I've found that the more I do something, the more it sticks. I also try not to beat myself

MY DISNEY OBSESSION

My family and I have been going to Disney World since I was five; we've been there a total of nine times (so far!). For me, Disney represents total escape. When I'm there, I literally forget about the real world and just lose myself in the magic and make-believe. My overthinking brain truly goes on holiday.

When I'm home, I try to capture that feeling by watching lots of Disney movies. My current favourite is *Moana*. First of all, *that soundtrack*! I listen to it on repeat. Also, I want so badly to live in Hawaii. Also, I love the main character. I love how strong and independent she is; she doesn't need a prince or anyone else to save her—she saves herself. I can relate to her because I've had moments of others putting me down, and I become completely discouraged . . . but then I reflect on all the things I've done and that I'm grateful for, and I think: "*I can do this.*"

Goofy introduced me to M&M'S when I was two. The love is real.

up if I stay up too late or succumb to a mid-morning bowl of ice cream or skip my evening face regimen once in a while. I aim for doing the best I can, which is still way better than my former YOLO approach to self-care.

(Confession: normally when I come home, I'm hungry, so I'll grab something healthy like an orange or cucumber slices. And then I'll think, "Now I can treat myself to a tiny, itty-bitty taste of raw Toll House cookie dough." And my sensible self will say: "DO NOT EAT THAT RAW COOKIE DOUGH." I come very close to listening to my sensible self, but then I shake my head and say, "I'm sorry, I have to", and reach for the spoon.)

I try to make sure to build in daily R&R time, too. Even if I only have twenty minutes between this VIP appointment and that VIP meeting and I'm already running late . . . even if I have six hours of stuff I absolutely need to accomplish today, and I only have three hours . . . I take a break. I close my eyes, do deep yoga breaths and think: "I can do this day." I let my brain have a rest. Or I drink a glass of water or make myself a cup of tea. Or I rub some lavender lotion on my hands. These little things can make a big difference. Afterwards, I'm like, "All right, I took my break, I can do my work again."

At night, especially if I've had a marathon day and have an early call time the next morning, I usually want to collapse into bed with my clothes and shoes on and just pass out. Or I'll force myself to stay up a little longer and catch up on my work e-mails. On those occasions, I have to remind myself that I need to decompress before I go to sleep because I will sleep better and wake up more refreshed.

And so I'll watch an episode of *Reign*. (For me, *Reign* is like *Pretty Little Liars* in medieval times, with pretty dresses. Pure escape. I'll watch it on my phone or laptop, depending on which device will die sooner and needs immediate charging.) Or I'll treat myself to a bubble bath.

Short Story

by Chloe Lukasiak

This is another short story I wrote for school. I tried to write it in the style of Ernest Hemingway and J. D. Salinger.

Today is the day my life changes. I grow up. I become an adult. The last day of my childhood. It's scary, you know? I graduate today and I have mixed emotions about it. What's going to happen tomorrow? Will I feel different? Probably not since I don't actually leave my parents' house till next week. I feel like most people don't leave right away, either. You know? I've dreamed of this day my whole life—I feel like everyone has. The day you graduate. Apparently it's a big day. I wouldn't know. Well, I won't know if it actually is. Not until tonight. You know? I'm excited to start a new chapter of my life. Maybe things will be different. I have a feeling life will get harder before it gets easier. Tomorrow is my first day of adulthood. No more high school. No more school dances. No more Friday night football games with themes. I will miss that stuff. But I probably won't miss the mean kids, the bullies, the early mornings every single day. I feel like a lot of people won't. You know? I was always so excited for high school when I was little. I just couldn't wait for it. And then when I got to high school, I couldn't wait for college. And I'm sure when I get to college, I'll be excited for the next step. Never really appreciating the moment I'm in now. Always wanting more, waiting for the next thing. You know? Today I am going to stop that cycle. I will appreciate my last moments with this group of people. I will appreciate walking onto that stage and them telling me, "Congratulations, you did it." I will live in that moment. Because I think it's really sad how we all forget to live in the moment. To put all of your focus and attention on what is happening right in front of you. You know? I guess that's the one thing I learned from high school. The one life lesson, I mean. You learn so much about the cells inside a plant or how to graph a function, but they forget to teach you about life. So you have to teach yourself. Or sometimes some people never learn. You know? And then you go off to college and you learn about the major you chose and it's some more sitting in a classroom, listening to teachers talk for hours and hours. It is different, though, because that's your major, that's what you chose. So you should enjoy it, right? I guess, but what if you didn't want to go to college? What if your parents forced you? I'm not saying mine did. I'm just saying IF. I wish someone would teach you a few things about life. But they never really do. You just grow up and teach yourself. Or you make a few mistakes and learn what NOT to do next time. You know? I guess that happens in high school, too. But there is more you have to learn after high school. You become independent, you're on your own. It's kind of scary. You know? I feel like one day I might miss the bullies and the early mornings. Probably not. Definitely not right now. But I'm just saying maybe. But you move on, you grow, you struggle. It's life. You know? I am scared for what's to come next. I'm also excited. But I am also living in the moment. Today I graduate and then I enter adulthood. I will walk onto that stage and appreciate being with this group of people one last time. Then I will say goodbye. I will enter the next chapter of my life. That's what life is. Experiencing something and then letting it go. Moving on to the next thing. You know?

A good hike can almost always put a smile back on my face.

With my overthinking brain, I find myself worrying about college and the future a lot these days. I know it's normal for teenagers to worry about this stuff. And I'm also really excited about what my future may hold. But sometimes, I forget to live in the present and just enjoy the Now. I think it's important to do that; otherwise, your life will pass you by.

GIVE YOURSELF PERMISSION TO CRY

I think I've cried about fifty times while filming *Dance Moms* these past months; a lot of memories, a lot of emotions have been stirred up. Sometimes I get mad at myself for crying. I tell myself to stop being a crybaby and to put on a brave face.

But then I remind myself that it's OK to cry. One hundred percent OK.

I hope you can give yourself permission to cry, too. Being able to cry means that you have a soft, tender heart in a difficult and sometimes cruel world.

I know that it's not always easy, and maybe sometimes, the despair is so deep and relentless that you want to just give up. But please don't. You have to keep going. And I know this sounds so much easier than it is. Trust me, I've been in dark places. We all have. I still sometimes go there.

Just let the tears flow until you feel better, then wipe them away and face the day. And know that whatever is making you cry, whoever is making you cry, can't take away the light in you. *You* are the light.

Or I'll read a book in my favourite comfy chair. Or, at the very least, I'll light a candle, lie down and take some deep breaths. Even five minutes of me time before bedtime is an essential daily habit to keep things serene (or at least sane).

This may sound counter-intuitive, but I'm also a huge believer in lists as a way to manage the stress. Lists keep me grounded and also focused on the tasks I need to accomplish. I always try to rate the tasks by importance and also arrange them in an efficient way . . . like, if I need to do an errand but my mom won't be home until later to drive me, I will use that time to knock off the little things on my list.

Call me a dork, but I will actually write "BREAK" on my to-do list. Because I consider breaks to be as important as the busy-work. Like:

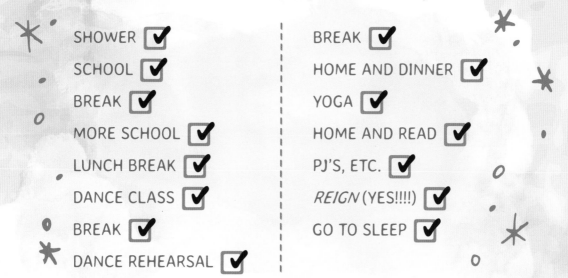

SHOWER ✔

SCHOOL ✔

BREAK ✔

MORE SCHOOL ✔

LUNCH BREAK ✔

DANCE CLASS ✔

BREAK ✔

DANCE REHEARSAL ✔

BREAK ✔

HOME AND DINNER ✔

YOGA ✔

HOME AND READ ✔

PJ'S, ETC. ✔

REIGN (YES!!!!) ✔

GO TO SLEEP ✔

If ever I start panicking because I'm trying to do twelve things at once and nothing is getting accomplished, I make myself stop, take a deep breath (yes, I know, there is a lot of deep breathing in this chapter—because it works!), and focus on just one task. Then, if I manage to finish that task, I pat myself on the back: *Yay, I got something done!* It's important to be positive and to acknowledge progress, even if it's baby-step progress. And it's equally important to not be mean to yourself.

You can only do what you can do. Be kind to yourself.

(OK, now for that bowl of Half Baked ice cream . . .)

CHAPTER 18

Time to Celebrate!

get dazzled

At Chloe & Nia's
11th birthday party

FRIDAY, JUNE 1ST
AT 7:00 PM

RSVP by May 29th

One of my favorite birthday celebrations was when I turned eleven. Nia and I have birthdays close to each other—I'm May 25 and she's June 20—so that year, we decided to have a party together. We had it at my house; my parents got a huge tent for our backyard, and we put a dance floor down. There was a DJ, lots of cool lights, and the cutest cake with sparkler candles!

I love holidays and other celebrations. I'm that girl who will kick off the "holiday season" in September, or whenever it is that Starbucks begins serving pumpkin spice lattes, and celebrate all the way through to New Year's Day. I totally get why some people celebrate "birthday weeks" or even "birthday months".

(Umm . . . excuse me while I make a little note in my calendar to block out the entire month of May this year. JK!)

Like my Disney obsession, these special times allow me to escape from the real world and indulge in pure happiness, pure pleasure. During holidays and celebrations, all problems are put on hold until further notice.

At the same time, I like to keep things simple and focus on being with my friends and family. For Halloween, I love staying at home and passing out candy to the adorable little kids in their costumes. (My friends prefer going to parties, which leads me to joke with them that I'm the "grandma" of my generation, LOL.) My last Halloween was pretty chill—I baked Halloween cookies and did schoolwork, and then, after Clara went to sleep, my mom and dad and

The birthday queens!

I watched *Scream*. (Some of us closed our eyes and covered our ears a lot. Not saying who.) The Halloween before that, I was in Vancouver

Nothing can scare me away from the Halloween candy!

filming *Center Stage*, so there wasn't time to do much celebrating besides going to a candy store with Amy, a family friend, and buying chocolate-covered strawberries and marshmallows and milk chocolate truffles. I was glad to be with her and to be filming the movie, but at the same time, I really missed being home!

Thanksgiving is also pretty chill, usually dinner with the extended family at our house or at the house of one of our relatives. I'm kind of a picky eater, so I'm not that into all the turkey and stuffing and other

Thanksgiving dishes. I *do* have a very important requirement, though, which is that I have to watch all the Thanksgiving episodes from *Friends* (including the infamous Monica one) no matter where I am. It's like how some people are glued to the TV set watching football games on Thanksgiving Day . . . For me, it's Ross and Rachel and the gang on my phone or laptop.

This one or that one?

Or maybe all of them?

EMBARRASSING VACATION STORY

My family loves going on beach holidays, and sometimes, we'll rent a big house with our aunts and uncles and cousins (especially my cousins Dylan, Katie and Emma). The parents get the bedrooms and the kids end up sleeping in the living room in our sleeping bags. We swim, we boogie-board, we make s'mores on a fire . . . It's tons of fun!

One summer, though, it wasn't so fun. The adults arranged for some kind of activity for the kids that involved going out on a small, sandy island with a tour guide. Once there, the guide told us to wade out in the water; I think we were supposed to catch stuff in the water.

But it turned out that the water was full of stingrays. Like, *dozens* of them. I refused to leave the island.

"Just shuffle your feet and they won't sting you," the tour guide told me. He waved his arm to indicate all the other kids who were in the water, shuffling their feet and having a grand old time. How was no one else terrified of being stung?

I wouldn't budge. For two whole hours. I stood there, marooned, while the other kids did the activity!

At Tiffany's in NYC, getting some ideas for Christmas.

TRAVEL

WISH LIST

I've been lucky enough to visit many wonderful places, including France, England, Ireland, Scotland, Australia, New Zealand, Mexico, Canada, Jamaica, Aruba, Puerto Rico and all over the United States—not every single state, but a lot of them.

I've started a wish list of places I'd like to visit in the future: Greece, Thailand, the Maldives, Bora-Bora, Germany and Italy. Honestly, I would love nothing more than to travel all over the world. I plan on visiting lots and lots of places in the future!

Christmas is probably my favourite holiday, partly because our family has a bunch of traditions that we repeat year after year—they're our bond, our history. One of my favourite Lukasiak traditions happens on the day before Christmas Eve (aka "Christmas Eve Eve"). We always have dinner at this fancy restaurant called Ruth's Chris Steak House and then we see the *Nutcracker* ballet in Pittsburgh, performed by the Pittsburgh Ballet Theatre company. (This past Christmas, Clara added to the family tradition by appearing in her very first *Nutcracker* with her studio, the Wexford Dance Academy. She played an angel!)

Rockefeller Center!

When Gram was alive, I shared some sweet little Christmas traditions with her. Like I would arrange her toy train set around her Christmas tree, and we would make these yummy treats called peanut butter blossoms. Whenever I make them now, just the smell of them

PEANUT BUTTER BLOSSOMS

THIS IS HOW OUR FAMILY MAKES PEANUT BUTTER BLOSSOMS.

Set the oven to 375°F.

Make your favourite peanut butter cookie dough recipe. You'll also need a bag of Hershey's Kisses and a bowl of sugar.

Take the dough and roll pieces of it into medium-size balls (or small ones, depending on how big you want your cookies to be).

Roll the balls in the sugar.

Place the balls on a cookie sheet.

Let them bake for about 15 minutes, or until you think they smell done; smaller cookies cook faster. (Honestly, we often just wing it.)

Take them out of the oven and remove them from the cookie sheet to cool a little.

Before the cookies set completely, put a Hershey's Kiss in the middle of each.

Ta-da!

JK, Santa! Bring on the presents!

transports me back to those wonderful times. I miss her so much, but at the same time I can still feel her love as I recall the traditions she and I shared.

I guess that's the whole point of traditions: sharing something meaningful with the people you love.

One of my favourite presents I ever gave was home-made; Clara and I made them together for our parents. We took two jars, one for Mom and one for Dad; I painted the jars red, tied them with pretty green ribbons, and attached gift tags that said: "50 REASONS I LOVE YOU." We filled each jar with fifty reasons why we loved them.

THE SECOND-BEST
CHRISTMAS PRESENT EVER

One Christmas, Mom and Dad surprised Clara and me with a mystery present. (I'm a big fan of surprises. Also mysteries. Also presents.) Nestled on the branches of our Christmas tree was ... wait for it ... a *clue*.

Now, my parents normally just give us our presents the old-fashioned way, i.e. wrapped in shiny red-and-green paper and tucked under the tree. And there *were* those presents; I remember because I made myself open them sloooowly and savour each one (versus tearing through them like a five-year-old, which is my usual M.O.).

But in addition to the many boxes and gift bags, there was that clue: a note on cream paper with red-and-gold writing. This was new and different and exciting!

The clue said:

Dear Chloe and Clara,
You've both been very good this year.
For this last gift, you will have to work a little harder.

That clue went on, describing what turned out to be the deck above our pool. There were more clues along the way that we had to follow.

Of course, Clara and I fought and argued to see who could get to the clues first. (Very Christmas spirit of us.) Eventually, we decided to compromise and take turns, which was really hard for me because ... remember? I'm five years old.

Eventually we ended up at my awesome purple Teen Choice Award 2015 surfboard.

Near the surfboard was another clue:

Surf's up, dudes, almost time for warm cuddles.
Head back upstairs
Where the lights look like bubbles.

OK, so that was the laundry room upstairs that had bubble-shaped lights. That led us to Gram's pearl necklace, then a cool fish sculpture that we'd bought in Mexico, then the "queen's castle"—Clara's room, since she has posters from various princess movies on her walls, plus she's "the queen" (LOL!).

Eventually, we ended up in Mom's bathroom. Floating in the tub was a little inflatable boat. And inside the boat was our treasure—four tickets for a Disney Cruise in the Caribbean!

This was absolutely, positively the best Christmas present since my parents told me that I was going to have a little sibling! And the cruise, which we took a few weeks later, turned out to be one of the best holidays of my life.

Chlo!
Chlo!

See? I've always loved Christmas,

especially with my family!

Dyeing Easter eggs with my lil' sis!

Happy Fourth of July!

This picture was taken in Pittsburgh on

Christmas Eve Eve, right before dinner at Ruth's

Chris Steak House and *The Nutcracker!*

This is my fifteenth birthday party at Barton G.'s in L.A. You can't see them in the picture, but I'm with a bunch of people, including my mom, a few close friends, and some of the cast members from *A Cowgirl's Story* (because I was filming at the time).

My mom always said that it's the love in the home that matters, not the *stuff*. She's so right.

As I write this, my sixteenth birthday is right around the corner. I know that sixteen is a big deal and that I should probably be organizing some elaborate, once-in-a-lifetime event with limos and chocolate fountains and live circus animals or whatever. (JK!)

Honestly? I just want something simple, like a pool party with some cool lights and a nice cake. As long as I have my family and friends around me, it will be exactly the celebration I want!

CHAPTER 19

Kindness Is a Superpower

If I could make a change in the world...

people would all share their toys. Chloe

-Dr. Martin Luther King, Jr.

Some words of wisdom from five-year-old me.

*I*f I had to list all my personal goals in order, "Practise kindness" would be at the top of the list. I want to be a kinder person to others, and I want to be a kinder person to myself.

I truly believe that kindness is a superpower. It's transformative. It can create a positive ripple effect within you—in your mood, in your attitude, in your brain chemistry—and then ripple out into the world, touching the lives of friends, family members, acquaintances, strangers . . . and even enemies.

Just try this experiment. Stop whatever you're doing (um, I guess that would be reading this book?). Do one small, nice thing for yourself. Make a cup of your favourite tea. Or schedule a massage (and put it on your calendar with a big smiley face). Or take a bubble bath. Or simply give yourself a compliment ("I look nice in this sweater" . . . "I played my violin solo really well" . . . "I was crazy brave to jump off the high dive").

Can you feel it? The transformation? Maybe before, you were feeling a bit blah or grumpy. And maybe now, your heart feels a little lighter?

OK, the next step of the experiment is to do something nice for someone else. Like . . . tell your parents *you'll* make dinner tonight so

> Three things in human life are important. The first is to be kind. The second is to be kind. And the third is to be kind.
>
> —*Henry James* (author)

Talking to an editor from *Life and Style* magazine about the Elizabeth Glaser Pediatric AIDS Foundation.

they can relax. Or send an e-gift card to a faraway friend. Or let your sister borrow your favourite earrings. Or give a compliment to a person you've never complimented before.

Spread the kindness around and see what happens.

One obstacle I've always bumped into is the idea that kindness has to be earned or deserved. Like, why should I be nice to myself when I was lazy and didn't finish my schoolwork today like I was supposed to? Why should I be nice to my friend who forgot about our coffee date last weekend?

Helping a charity is one of the best ways to practise kindness. Find one that is close to your heart, whether it's teaching literacy, taking care of stray animals, fighting domestic violence, building schools for girls around the world, providing clean water to countries that don't have it . . . or one of the hundreds (if not thousands) of other worthy charities out there.

If it's a local charity, you might volunteer weekly or monthly for that organization, or you might volunteer for specific events (like offering to assist with a fundraising party). Donating is another way to help; give what you can, even if it's just five or ten pounds, or talk to the headteacher (or a teacher) at your school or your boss at work to find out how you can organize (or participate in) a group-giving effort. Spreading information about a cause (whether via social media or word of mouth) is also a great way to get involved.

I've helped raise money for the Children's Miracle Network, which benefits patients in children's hospitals around the country. I support Children's Hospital of Pittsburgh of UPMC because I was a patient there and am very grateful for the wonderful care I got. For me, there is nothing more important than helping sick kids. One of our biggest fundraisers is the Walk for Children's each year.

> The level of our success is limited only by our imagination and no act of kindness, however small, is ever wasted.
>
> —*Aesop* (storyteller)

The Moon

by Chloe Lukasiak

In addition to loving the stars, I also love the moon. Basically, I've always been intrigued by everything to do with the sky and the night. When I decided to write this poem, the words just came to me. I was struck by how the moon (like the stars) brightens the darkness—not just the *actual* darkness but emotional and spiritual darkness, too.

The Nickelodeon HALO Awards show with Clara.

The moon was the mother of the night,

She watched over her children with care,

The stars came out to bring light,

She loved all of them equal and fair,

Some argued about how she came to be so bright,

But it didn't matter, for in the night, she was a prayer.

For attractive lips, speak words of kindness.

For lovely eyes, seek out the good in people.

—*Sam Levenson*
(writer and journalist)

Nope, nope, nope. Kindness first . . . grinding on flaws, short-comings and disappointments second (or better yet, not at all). Kindness isn't a reward one receives for having checked off all the items on the checklist. Kindness is unconditional. That's part of what makes it a superpower!

Kindness is also compassionate. The Dalai Lama said, "If you want others to be happy, practise compassion. If you want to be happy, practise compassion." Sometimes I have to remind myself that other people have stuff going on that I know nothing about. Maybe my friend forgot about our coffee date because she overheard her parents talking about a divorce. And maybe last week when somebody bumped into me on the street and was rude to me, it's because she was worried about her sick cat. We should all try to err on the side of compassion. Looking through the lens of compassion will automatically make *us* less annoyed, and the other person feel less judged and criticized.

I was one of the runway models for a fashion show hosted by BCBG Max Azria to benefit the Make-a-Wish Foundation. Here I am with fashion designer Lubov Azria.

This may sound weird, but . . . I sometimes also use kindness to sur-prise and disarm the other person. For example, say someone insults me. Instead of getting upset, I might just give them a warm, friendly smile and say, "Oh, by the way, I really loved your short story in English class! You're a great writer." This type of response will often confuse and unravel the other person and either render them speechless or force them to smile and return the kindness. Sneaky, I know—but it's definitely using my superpower for good!

I asked my mom the other day if she thought I was a kind person, and she said yes (because she's my mom, LOL). She pointed out all the everyday ways in which I am kind to people, whether I'm aware of them or not. She said that I always try to be nice to everyone, I'm super polite to "children and the elderly" (her words), I overtip at restaurants, and I smile at strangers. I'm also involved in various charities, including one that's especially important to me (see page 175).

BE KIND TO VICTIMS OF BULLIES

I mentioned in chapter 7 that it's important to be kind to victims of bullies. Victims of bullies—depending on their situation—often feel isolated, insecure, stressed out, frightened, depressed or even suicidal. Just making sure they know they're not alone, that there are people who care about them and want to support them, can be a big help and comfort.

(If you think the person is in danger, though, please call 999 IMMEDIATELY; and if the person seems suicidal, IMMEDIATELY tell an adult and also IMMEDI-ATELY call 999 or the Samaritans Helpline on 116 123 - UK and ROI.)

I've been working on other ways to cultivate everyday kindness. Here are some ideas I came up with. Maybe they'll inspire you, too?

- Take a friend out for coffee or lunch or dinner, just because.
- Send someone flowers (no special occasion necessary).
- Leave a book for a stranger to pick up and read, like on a park bench or a subway seat. You can even leave an anonymous little note or bookmark inside saying: "Enjoy this book!" or "A gift from a fellow bookworm!"
- Offer to babysit for a neighbor or family friend.
- Thank someone if they are kind to you. Keep the kindness ripple effect going.
- Hold the door open for people.
- Let someone else go first.
- If you're in a long line, offer to switch spots with the harried parent in the back of the line who's trying to calm down three wriggly kids.
- Buy a box of blank notecards and a bunch of stamps. Then send people handwritten notes, whether thank-you notes or "Hi, I'm thinking about you" notes or "I'm sorry for that thing I did; can we be friends again?" notes.
- Spend time with a senior citizen who lives alone, just hanging out and talking or helping them with chores and errands.
- If you feel like complaining to someone about something they did, take a second to reconsider . . . and maybe let it slide.
- Buy a bunch of gift cards from carry-out restaurants and grocery stores and hand them out to homeless people.

- Thank people—not just the ones you usually thank but the ones you never thank. Thank the cafeteria lady; thank the mail carrier; thank the receptionist at your dentist's office.

- Forgive old grudges.

- Forgive debts, like if someone owes you money because you paid for their movie last weekend.

- If you're at a party or other event and there's a person who looks like she doesn't know anyone, go up to her and introduce yourself.

- Call, e-mail, or text someone you haven't talked to in a while.

- Give someone a gift anonymously.

- Practice kindness when you're in a bad mood.

- Be kind to someone you don't like.

- Smile.

- Smile some more.

- Keep smiling.

I'm sure I'll keep adding to this list, and if you have any good suggestions, please send them along!

So, yeah. Spread kindness, you guys. Let's make it our mission.

CHAPTER 20

Taking On the World

MARGARET AND MARGARITA

COURAGE

I am brave when I hear bears growl at the zoo.

Chloe

I made this in preschool!

*T*o take on the world, start with just one small thing. No big, grand actions. No leaps across the abyss. No life-altering decisions.

Just one small thing.

This is a variation on one of the themes I've been talking about throughout the book. Life can be overwhelming. A single *day* can be overwhelming. If I sat here at my desk and thought about all the challenges I have going on right now, the stuff on my to-do list that was due yesterday, I would . . . quit. Or hide. Or burst into tears. Or all of the above.

I totally understand about panic. We all panic about temporary or situational problems, like: "Oh my gosh, the history test is tomorrow? I thought it was NEXT Thursday!" Or: "What do you mean I won't be able to dance for a couple of months?" Or: "I am going to be sooo late for my important audition!" Or: "I totally forgot my friend's birthday!"

Then there are the big, existential crises like: "My family and friends think that my dreams and goals are crazy. Are they right?" Or: "I have no idea what I want to do with my life. I'm not really passionate about anything." Or: "I hate college." Or: "I'm unhappy, and I don't know how to fix my unhappiness."

I'm ready to tackle my day!

TIPS FOR GETTING YOUR BUTT OUT OF BED IN THE MORNING

Tackling the world starts with getting out of bed, which needless to say is not always easy. Here are some tips that work for me (*most of the time . . . the rest of the time, well, my bed is sooo comfy!*).

(BTW, to get your butt out of bed in the morning, you actually have to start with the night before, so the first five tips are for night-time.)

✳ As much as possible (and it's not always possible for me), have a consistent bedtime. That, along with a consistent wake-up time, will set your body's natural rhythms and make it easier to both fall asleep *and* wake up.

✳ Make sure you have a cosy sleeping space. For me, that means my Tempur-Pedic pillow (my neck is a little sensitive and can easily cramp up), my crisp white sheets and my big, cosy duvet. (I used to have sparkly lights covering the doorway to my bathroom, but my parents made me take them down because they said they were too bright for night-time, which I never understood, but oh well.) Also, I like to light a candle before bedtime; when I blow it out, I can fall asleep with that scent in my room.

✳ Lay out your outfit for tomorrow and organize your handbag or backpack or whatever you carry your stuff in.

✳ Make a list of what you want to accomplish tomorrow. But keep it simple; you don't want to wake up to an overwhelming, mile-long to-do list! I do this on a reminder app on my phone.

✳ Then turn off the technology! Screens affect your brain and keep it from wanting to fall asleep. Read a book instead . . . It's scientifically proven to unwind your mind! I also like to write in my journal right before lights out.

✳ When the alarm goes off in the morning, smile! That's right . . . smile. Even if you had a bad night full of tossing and turning and dreams about evil clowns chasing you through the basement. That smile will fill your body with happy vibes and get your day off to a positive start.

✻ Look out your window and say "Good morning!" to the morning. Find something interesting or beautiful to admire about this particular morning, whether it's the pink and gold of the sunrise or the soft grey misty rain or your cat sitting on your chest and staring at you intently with that "I'm hungry, what are you going to do about it?" look.

✻ Keep some nice wake-up aromatherapy on your bedside table. Peppermint, rosemary, cinnamon, grapefruit and orange are really energizing; you can get bottles of essential oils, candles, lotions and other products in these scents.

✻ Do some light stretches in bed. While lying down, point your toes and stretch your arms over your head and make yourself as looong as you can. It will wake up your body!

✻ I've started *not* reaching for my phone the second I'm awake. Instead, I make myself a cup of Earl Grey lavender tea and sit in my chair by the window for five to ten minutes, just thinking about all the things I'm grateful for and also the goals I want to accomplish for the day.

✻ Have a playlist of happy or energizing or calming or whatever-you-need-in-the-morning music to start your day. Keep listening as you make your bed (this is a must because then you can't climb back into bed so easily!), go to the bathroom, take a shower and get dressed. Feel free to dance!

✻ Eat a good breakfast that will fuel your mind and body. My favourite breakfast is eggs, bacon, fruit, toast, OJ and tea. Some days I will change it up and have maple and brown sugar oatmeal. If I'm in a rush, I will grab an apple and a banana. I always feel like if I eat breakfast, I've accomplished something, and I can get on with my day.

✻ I like to plan one nice thing that's just for me, every day. That way, if I "wake up on the wrong side of the bed" (I totally get that expression now!) and am all grumpy and tired and "I-just-want-to-go-back-to-sleep-can't-the-world-just-leave-me-alone?", I can remind myself of that one nice thing to look forward to, whether it's a smoothie or ice cream or baking cookies or going shopping with my mom or painting my toenails with my new apple-red or baby-pink nail polish.

✻ Remember that awesome phrase "I can do this day"? Say it a few more times. Repeat as necessary.

If all else fails, fake it till you make it!

ANIMATION IS ACTING, DAHLING.

Whether your problem is big, little or in between, my advice is . . . cancel the panic. Unless you're being chased by the proverbial lion (in which case you *need* your stress hormones to go into overdrive so you can function in fight-or-flight mode), panic is a waste of your time and energy. If you *have* to panic about something, allow yourself like a five- or ten-minute freak-out period . . . then move on. Do that one small thing that will shift your emotional gears into a productive place. It might be (and I know this may sound silly, but bear with me) moving into a different room. Or opening a window and feeling the cool breeze on your face. Or changing your socks. Or . . .

OK, so you're probably thinking: "Um, Chloe? You're supposed to be teaching me how to take on the world, and you're telling me to put on different *socks*?"

No. And yes. The point is, it's these little things that can move us from non-action to action, from despair to determination. Baby steps, remember? If you're sitting in your room just kind of frozen in place because you don't know how to solve your problem or get started with your new goal, then change your socks, drink a glass of water, take a life-changing shower, call a friend, eat an apple, go for a walk . . . something, *anything*. That baby step will lead to another baby step and so on and so on . . . and before you know it, a solution, a plan will reveal itself to you like a ray of sunshine cutting through the grey fog.

I remember, after my mom and I left *Dance Moms* in 2014, I was in a bad place physically, mentally and emotionally. I felt lost, unmoored from the life I had known for so many years. I spent a lot of time lying in bed and watching TV and not knowing where to go or what to do next.

FINDING
YOUR PASSION

Some people seem to find their passions early in life and have a plan and a dream in place. But if you're not one of those people, don't worry—you're not alone. Read about anything and everything. Take tons of classes. Have adventures. Your passion will come to you.

I didn't grand jeté from the last day of Season Four to my decision to keep dancing and to try acting as well. There was a lot of anxiety and panic and uncertainty in between.

It was the baby steps that kept me moving forward. (That, and my wonderful family and also counselling.) I went through a series of life-changing showers and other micro-accomplishments (eating a healthy breakfast on Monday, going for a walk around the neighbourhood on Tuesday, totally backsliding and being a useless blob on Wednesday, picking up a new novel on Thursday, researching yoga classes on Friday, watching a Cate Blanchett movie on Saturday, and so on . . .) that slowly, gradually, eventually led me to that ray of sunshine.

Smile!

So.

You *will* take on the world. But you don't have to take on the *whole* world today.

For today, this is your assignment:

- ♥ Do one small thing. Accomplish a microgoal.
- ♥ Believe in yourself.
- ♥ Be kind to yourself (and to others).
- ♥ Smile even if you don't feel like smiling. (Your mood will catch up later.)
- ♥ Say to yourself: "I can do this day."

Everything Happens for a Reason

Me before my first solo performance, "Baby Mine," on *Dance Moms.*

So now I've returned to *Dance Moms* and started competing again. I've reconnected with wonderful old friends and met new friends, too. I've continued with my acting, dancing and YouTube. I've been setting some new goals for myself (like learning how to play the piano!).

When I was back on the *Dance Moms* set after all these years, I had this epiphany. It occurred to me that I probably grew up too fast the first time around, being around adults all the time, witnessing so much conflict and drama, and also having so many expectations placed on me at such a young age.

But . . . growing up too fast might have been a positive, too, because all the things I learned and experienced during that stage of my life helped me make better decisions later on.

MY WRITING
PLAYLIST

Here are some songs I've been listening to while working on this book:

⭐ "Lower Your Eyelids to Die with the Sun" by M83

⭐ "You've Got the Love" by Florence + the Machine

⭐ "Cosmic Love" by Florence + the Machine

⭐ "Moonchild" by M83

⭐ "Wait" by M83

⭐ "Breezeblocks" by Δ (alt-J)

Dreaming of making it big in L.A.

I look back at that time, and part of me wishes that the fifteen-year-old me could tell the younger me everything I know now. If I could somehow travel back in time and go through that experience again, I would make different choices, see things differently.

But I guess that's the point of maturity.

This is how much I've changed. This is how much I've grown up. I can practically measure my growth in memories—good memories *and* bad memories.

Honestly, though? I wouldn't trade any of them.

Because everything happens for a reason.

I love where I am today, right here, right now. And I wouldn't be here if it hadn't been for the conflict and drama, the pain, the challenges.

Speaking of the future . . .

So I've recently also been visiting colleges. My mom and I toured USC; it was awesome, their film school was so beautiful, and I was like, "I want to go here *now*, and I want to learn all about scriptwriting and directing and producing, and continue with my dance, and maybe take

My friend Sarah Reasons and I are attending an info session, which is part of the USC tour.

Will I be a USC Trojan in the future?

some pre-med courses, and . . . wait, *what*? They have a class on *STAR WARS*?" I'm also checking out UCLA and UC Santa Barbara and some East Coast schools, too.

For now, I'll continue with *Dance Moms* and dance and acting. And my schoolwork. And I'm so excited to get my driver's licence!

I have so much to be thankful for and so much to look forward to.

OK, so now that we're nearing the end of the book, I want to say something to you all.

Thank you. Thank you for sharing this journey with me. Thank you for indulging my dorky sense of humor. Thank you for letting me into your life with my words. And thank you, too, to those who have supported me and sent me kind words over the years.

I hope I've helped you with this book. I hope it's given you strength and hope and laughter. I hope, too, that you know you're not alone. We are a community, an ensemble—take my hand, and let's embark on the crazy adventure of life together!

And don't forget:

Believe in yourself.

Be kind to yourself.

Love you all,

THE END!

AND THE DANCER
GIRL GRAND JETÉD
INTO THE SUNSET!

Peace out, people!

Ummm . . .

I thought that was the end of the book, but it's not! Guys, my family and friends surprised me by sending in a bunch of stories about me to my publisher. I'm so honoured . . . and a little nervous, because what if they said embarrassing stuff about me? Gah! Well, anyway, enjoy!

Marc Lukasiak (father)

I can vividly remember the day Chloe was born (which is saying something, because I have a terrible memory). Christi and I were in a private room at the hospital. She had been in labour for forty hours, but still no baby. I was sitting by her side and reading a magazine and just waiting and waiting with her.

The doctors decided to help speed things up, so they gave Christi medication to induce labour. A few minutes later they wheeled her out of there; all they told me was that it was an emergency and they needed to move quickly. So suddenly I'm in the room by myself with no idea what's happening.

Some time goes by (maybe less than an hour, but it felt like more) and the doctors came back in to talk to me. They told me that the baby's umbilical cord had been wrapped around her neck, and when they tried to induce labour, it caused complications because her air supply was being shut off. That's why they'd had to do an emergency operation, a C-section, to get the baby out of there.

A few minutes later Christi was wheeled back into the room, and I got to meet Chloe, who was fine and healthy. From her first day, I knew she would have a flair for the dramatic.

Kathy Lukasiak (grandmother)

My very earliest memory of Chloe was the day she was born. We had travelled to Pittsburgh for the birth, but they ended up sending us home because nothing was happening. After we arrived home, took a nap, and went to dinner, Christi called saying we needed to return to the hospital.

By the time we arrived, Chloe had been born. It was around 9:00 p.m., and we could hear her the moment we reached the maternity ward. We just followed the noise and found them. By the time we got there, Chloe had stopped crying and was sucking her thumb.

Marc Lukasiak (again!)

I have another very poignant memory of Chloe, from when she was five years old. Christi and I took her to Disney World for her fifth birthday, and it was just the three of us (this was before Clara was born). It is one of my favourite memories ever because Chloe was at that perfect age when everything there was magical for her, and everywhere we went, people wished her happy birthday and sang to her. She was just so incredibly happy, and I can still see that smile on her face. I think that trip started her lifelong love of all things Disney.

Kathy Lukasiak (again!)

One year, eleven of us went to the beach together for a family holiday. Chloe was six or seven years old. The cottage we rented happened to have a cupboard full of dance costumes. Chloe and her cousin Katie loved those costumes and performed many dance recitals for the adults during that holiday. I think that maybe Chloe was dreaming of being a professional dancer even then.

Throughout her childhood, she often came to visit us for the weekend. She and her cousins had so much fun together, swimming in our pool and playing with the little motored Jeep. After these weekends, I would often find notes and letters from Chloe that she had left for me, usually hidden (tucked among the toys in the playroom or written on the second page of a notepad). So heart-warming.

Kara Womer (aunt)

My favourite memory has to be when we were all in Ireland. Standing in front of the Blarney Castle, Chloe decided she wanted to do an aerial. She started to do one, then completely wiped out and smacked her face on the ground. After we made sure she wasn't hurt, we all laughed. Chloe was even able to laugh at herself.

BRittany Pent (family friend)

I've known Chloe since she was about five years old. I was a teenager at the time, but I always loved arriving early to dance competitions to see the girls perform their solos, duets and trios. Watching Chloe onstage was the absolute best! She always had the most incredible personality, and she stole my heart early on. I grew to love her like she was my own sister. Whenever I showed up at the dance studio, Chloe would scream my name, run up to me, and give me a gigantic hug. I look at her today, the beautiful young woman that she is, and can hardly believe how quickly she has grown before my own two eyes . . . and still she runs to me and gives me that gigantic hug.

Over the years, I travelled with Chloe and her mom to meet-and-greet events and to teach master dance classes all around the United States. You wouldn't believe the love that Chloe received, even from the smallest towns. Hundreds of kids would be lined up in front of hotels with big signs and gifts as she arrived. I remember this one time when we drove up to an event, and kids were screaming in excitement. Chloe leaned over to me and said, "Who's here? Who are they screaming for?" Giggling, I said, "Chloe, they're screaming for you!" She couldn't believe it. She's always been so humble.

As her fan base grew, we began to travel to other countries around the world. I remember an event in Australia, watching the kids go wild as Chloe and Christi arrived in a water taxi. The excitement Chloe sparked was incredible! These kids looked up to her; they adored her.

I commend Chloe for always being such an awesome role model, on and off the stage. She works hard, she stays humble and she is always sweet as can be.

There is one incident that always comes to mind when I think of Chloe and me as little kids. She and I were in the kitchen stealthily looking for snacks. We opened the bread bin and found some crumbs, and we were convinced that those crumbs meant there was a mouse lurking somewhere in the house.

We went back up to Chloe's room and piled every single one of her stuffed animals onto her bed to protect them from the evil mouse that may or may not have existed. We also decided to set a trap (aka a box on the floor beside her bed, tipped over on its side).

After the trap was ready to go, we climbed onto her bed, butterfly nets in hand, and waited for the mouse to appear. We sat there waiting for what felt like years. After a while, Chloe's mom walked into the room. She took one look at us surrounded by all of Chloe's stuffed animals, and at our fierce expressions as we stared down at our "mousetrap".

"Um, what on earth are you two doing?" she asked.

She tried to convince us that there was no mouse to catch, and even if there was, this wasn't the way to catch it. But Chloe wouldn't give up. She was determined to apprehend the dastardly mouse, even if it was quite literally impossible.

In 2009, my husband, Matt, and I moved to our new home in Churchill, Pennsylvania. As we were moving in, a little girl came bouncing out of the house next door followed by her very pregnant mother. The girl had long blonde hair and bright eyes. She was very polite, well spoken and was very curious as to who we were, but mostly she wanted to know if we had any children her age. After some brief introductions, we learned that the little girl's name was Chloe and she had just turned eight years old.

As we chatted with our new neighbours that day, we had no idea that in the year ahead, the whole world would discover just how special Chloe was, and that her life—her family's lives—would be changed forever.

Over the next year or so, our families became very close. We would often find Chloe swinging from the grapevines or perfecting her dancing skills in our back garden. One evening, Chloe was playing in our garden with her two-year-old sister, Clara, and my one-year-old daughter, Caroline. Chloe decided that she wanted to put on a circus show for the adults using Clara and Caroline as her "animals". The little girls loved that Chloe was giving them so much attention, and Chloe loved that she had younger children to boss around! Chloe trained the girls for their circus debut by jumping through hula hoops of "fire", walking the tightropes (which were actually skipping ropes), and roaring like lions. A few minutes into the show, Chloe lost control of her "circus animals" as they began doing somersaults and running around the garden. Chloe did her best to regain her control over the girls, but it was apparent the circus was over.

It was fun for us to watch a child who was growing up in front of cameras enjoy a simple evening with family and neighbours.

CLARA (sister)

I love spending time with Chloe and bonding over books. Chloe's a bookworm, and she's taught me to be one, too! She gives me book recommendations all the time. Right now, I am reading the *Sisters Grimm* series and am obsessed with it. I love talking to Chloe about these books and learning what she loved about them. We might be eight years apart, but it's still fun talking about the books we love.

HOLLY FRAZIER (Nia's mom)

One of my fondest memories was planning Nia and Chloe's eleventh birthday party with Christi. The girls' birthdays were just a few weeks apart, plus they wanted to invite many of the same guests, plus we all had these insanely busy travel schedules . . . so it made sense to have one fabulous celebration for the two of them.

We hired a party planner, and the rest was history. This party was unlike any other tween party we had ever seen. It was in Chloe's back garden, which had been transformed into a fun, chic L.A. setting and had pretty, twinkling lights. The atmosphere and vibe were electric . . . There was a fabulous three-tiered birthday cake, pic 'n' mix sweet table, photo booth and DJ. We couldn't stop dancing!

Nia FRAZIER (friend and Dance Moms teammate)

I was sleeping over at Chloe's house, and Paige [Hyland] was there, too. The night was filled with lots of fun, laughs and giggles. Part of any good sleepover involves a good beauty ritual or makeover, so we decided to do a mini spa treatment and give each other facials. We went to the kitchen to get the necessary ingredients for a DIY facial. Unfortunately, there was no Greek yoghurt or cucumbers, so we had to find substitutes. Trix yoghurt and courgette would have to do! We slathered yoghurt masks on our faces and put courgette slices on our eyelids. We discovered that, although tasty, Trix yoghurt and courgette are not the best DIY-facial substitutes. We also found out that it's important to clean up your mess in the kitchen before you go to bed, because who wants to do it in the morning?

Acknowledgments

Wow. Where do I even begin?

First, thank you so much to my BLOOMSbURY team, including Cindy Loh, Bethany Buck, Lizzy Mason, Cristina Gilbert, Erica Barmash, Beth Eller, Diane Aronson, Donna Mark, Melissa Kavonic, Cat Onder and Kay Petronio. I am so grateful to you all and am so honoured to have worked with you on my first book.

A SPeCiaL Shou+-ou+ +o MY COPY edi+OR, JiLL AMaCk. This book wouldn't be what it is without your incredible skill and care and thoughtfulness.

TO MY edi+OR, SuSan DObiniCk: Thank you so much for believing in my book and my message. Thank you for your kindness and your editorial wisdom. I owe you so much for making me a better writer and for having faith in me every step of the way.

TO MY Li+eRaRY agen+, An+hony Ma++eRO: Thank you for supporting my book from the beginning and for helping me through the entire process.

TO ALeX RiCe: Thank you for going above and beyond in pulling everything together.

TO John CoReLLa, BRYan S+inSOn, and KiM CheSSLeR: Thank you for the experience of a lifetime on *Dance Moms*. I will never forget it.

TO MY FRIENDS: Thank you for continuing to be there for me at every turn. You know who you are!

TO MY extended FAMILY: Thank you for your support in everything I do. Love you guys so much. And to Grammy Kathy and Papa D.: Thank you for your unconditional love. You're the best grandparents ever.

TO NANCY OHLIN: Thank you so much for everything you have done and for guiding me along the crazy path that is creating and publishing a book. I truly could not have done it without you. I can't believe we just wrote a book!!! (P.S. Clara Ohlin, you are beautiful and strong and brave. Never let anyone take away your bright light.)

TO MY PARENTS: Every single day, I am grateful that you are my parents. You keep me grounded, you teach me to be kind and you encourage me to stand up for what I believe in. You taught me to prove them wrong. Thank you for introducing me to my love of reading and writing. Also, thank you for putting up with me through my teen years. I hear it only gets better from here! I love you guys.

TO MY beautiful little sister: You make my days brighter and my laughs louder. You are my sister not just by blood, but by spirit. Thank you for believing in me, always. Keep your fiery heart, baby sis. I love you.

And to MY fans: There are no words that could do justice to the gratitude I feel for all of you. Thank you so, so much for all of your support and your unconditional love. Thank you for picking up this book and reading my story. Thank you for being there for me from the beginning of this journey. Thank you for having my back. I love each and every single one of you so much!

Thank you to everyone. I love you all.

OK, time to go pinch myself until I'm convinced this is real and not some wonderful dream.

About the Contributor

Nancy Ohlin was born in Tokyo and divided her childhood between there and Ohio. She is the author of the YA novels *Consent*, *Beauty* and *Always, Forever* as well as several series for young readers (*Greetings from Somewhere*, *Tales from Maple Ridge* and *Blast Back!*). She has collaborated on books with Quvenzhané Wallis (the *Shai & Emmie* series); Paige McKenzie (*The Sacrifice of Sunshine Girl*); and other celebrities. As a ghostwriter, she has published nearly a hundred titles for children, teens and adults. A graduate of the University of Chicago, she lives in Ithaca, New York, with her family. Learn more at nancyohlin.com.